INTENSIVE
Coursebook 3

Mark Ellis & Printha Ellis

COUNTERPOINT INTENSIVE COURSE
developed from Counterpoint General English Course
is based on a short course syllabus devised by

STEPHEN KEELER
Educational Consultant for
THAMES VALLEY
CULTURAL CENTRES

Nelson

CONTENTS

1
Sports beat
Describing actions and activities
Talking about unusual sports
page 1

2
Does the child make the man?
Making predictions
Talking about training and occupations
page 3

3
Clamping down on tourists
Asking for and giving explanations
Talking about parking regulations
page 5

4
Social situations
page 7

5
Say it with movements
Talking about how people look and feel
Comparing countries
page 9

6
Cash in on our service
Making suggestions
Talking about bank services
page 11

7
Becoming a woman in Japan
Talking about habit and custom
Agreeing and disagreeing
page 13

8
Find a new you at the Slim Inn
Giving varied descriptions
Discussing causes and results
page 15

9
Eurochick
Making and discussing proposals
page 17

10
Newspapers: How objective are they?
Discussing timetables
Interpreting headlines
page 19

11
Television
Expressing likes and dislikes
Talking about television viewing
page 21

12
Unlocking a legend
Expressing habit and frequency
Reporting commands
page 23

13
Seeing is believing
Expressing opinions
Expressing conflicting ideas
page 25

14
A magnificent obsession with colour
Talking about the past
Describing paintings
page 27

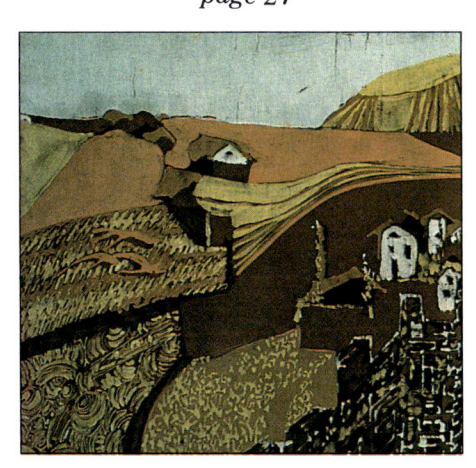

15
Colour talks
Giving explanations
Talking about colours
page 29

16
Operation Raleigh
Talking about the world
page 31

17
Adopt an animal at London Zoo
Explaining and describing emotions
Categorising animals
page 33

18
A kind of medicine
Talking about advantages and disadvantages
Giving advice
page 35

19
Movers: how mobile are you?
Giving information about people
Talking about travel
page 37

20
Missing
Talking about personal possessions
Affirming or denying emphatically
page 39

Exercises Units 1-20
page 41
Tapescript
page 61

SPORTS BEAT

We are all becoming more aware of our health and the importance of exercise, and many unusual sports are becoming very popular. More people are exploring caves under the sea, hanging from parachutes or riding the waves on a board – and they aren't all young, or rich, or even very good. Here's a brief look at some of the things on today's sports scene.

▲ **Underwater caving: Great Britain**

'Underwater caving is an adventure,' says Stewart Stone, 38. 'It's dangerous, but it's also very beautiful. Under the sea there is a completely new world of caves and you are discovering it.' Stewart usually works in a bank in Scotland but he practises diving every weekend. Here he is 'kitting up' – putting on his equipment. 'This new suit is a Viking,' he says. 'It's warmer than my old wetsuit. That's very important in the North Sea.' Good equipment is very important. But first you have to be an excellent diver.

▲ **Heli-skiing: British Columbia**

Andrea Lachen, 28, is a ski instructor from Gstaad, Switzerland, but here she is in the Canadian Rockies. 'British Columbia is the heli-ski capital of the world,' she says. 'I like heli-skiing because you are not skiing at a resort, with hundreds of other people. The helicopter takes you to the top and there are huge areas of unused powder – lovely light, dry snow. You can go down seven or eight times in a day.' Andrea says that it's a wonderful experience, but it's expensive and you have to be a good skier and in very good shape.

1 Read the text and the descriptions of the photographs, and match the words in Column **A** below with their meanings in Column **B**:

A	B
underwater caving	putting on equipment
parasailing	exploring caves under the sea
kitting up	made by hand
custom-made	hanging from a parachute attached to a boat
windsurfing	riding the waves on a board
in good shape	very healthy

2 Imagine that you are doing an interesting sport. Write a description of what you are doing. Now complete these questions to ask about your partner's sport:
1 What sport ___ chosen?
2 What are you ___?
3 Where ___?
4 Who ___?
5 What ___ wearing?

3 Ask and answer questions like this:
Isn't skiing dangerous?
–Yes, I think so./No, I don't think so.
Use: exciting boring expensive difficult easy safe

4 Write a sentence about a sport from experience, like this:
Diving is often dangerous./Windsurfing is easy.
Listen as other students say their sentences and write down one or two of them. Then ask questions like this:
Who said that diving was dangerous?
– John did.

5 Work in pairs and use the texts to complete sentences, like this:
A *If you're not a good diver, you can't . . . .*
B *If you're not a good diver, you can't go underwater caving.*
Use these phrases: good swimmer   good skier   in good shape   haven't got good equipment   haven't got much money   if it's windy

1

▲ **Windsurfing: Gran Canaria**

▲ **Parasailing: Poros**

Windsurfing is one of today's fastest growing sports and it's popular with all ages. Claude owns a windsurfing club in Antibes, but for his holidays he goes windsurfing in other places. This year he is going to Gran Canaria, and he is taking his board with him! 'It's an Open Class roundboard,' he says, 'very fast, and it's custom-made – very expensive, of course, because it's made by hand. A lot of people are flying out to the Canaries with their own boards these days.'

'I like water-skiing, so I run a water-skiing school. I combine business with pleasure,' says Photos Skivalos, 31. Here he is parasailing and his brother, Yannis, is driving the boat. 'A lot of people prefer parasailing,' Yannis says. 'They pay their money and we take them up for about fifteen minutes. It's not really a sport. They don't have to do anything.' Most Greek resorts offer parasailing, but be careful when you book – if it's windy you can't go up.

6 Make sentences from the table and say where you can find these things.

For example:
You can often find caves under the water/in the sea.

You can often find	caves parachutes divers windsurfers water-skiers ski resorts jockeys tobogganers helicopters	in under on behind above	the air. the water. the ground. mountains. horses. Switzerland. the sea. boards. boats.

7 Here are some facts about the people in the photographs. Listen to them talking on the tape and complete the chart below.

Name	Age	Lives in	Work	Free time activity
Andrea	28	Gstaad	teaches skiing	train for/Olympics
Photos	31	Poros	runs water-skiing school	
Yannis				
Claude		Antibes		
Stewart	38			

Make questions and answers using the table and the photographs:
What can you tell me about Andrea?
– Andrea is a 28-year-old woman who teaches skiing and is training for the Olympics.

SUMMARY

Now you can:
describe actions and activities

KEY GRAMMAR
Present continuous tense
We are all becoming more aware of our health.

Defining relatives: who
Andrea is a 28-year-old woman who teaches skiing.

First conditional + can
If you're not a good diver, you can't go underwater caving.

VOCABULARY
diving
heli-skiing
parasailing
underwater caving
water-skiing
windsurfing

board (surfboard)
cave
parachute
waves
wetsuit
custom-made
kit up

1

Max Jeffrey, orphan.
'I want to be a fighter. I'm going to be a boxer.'

Franny Campbell, daughter of a shopkeeper.
'I'm going to be like my mum.'

	Max	Franny
Marital status	married	married (at 17)
Children	5	2
Occupation	foreman/ frozen food factory	housewife
Feels	happy	very happy
Education	left school with 4 'O' levels	left school at 16/ no qualifications

DOES THE CHILD

Twenty years ago Robert Markham, a well-known sociologist, interviewed twenty children, all aged seven or eight. Some were from rich families, some from poorer families and some were middle class.

1 Listen to Robert Markham interviewing Jennifer. She is talking about her family and what she is going to be when she grows up. Write a caption to accompany her photograph.

2 Ask and answer in pairs like this:
What is Max going to do when he grows up?
– He's going to ___ .
What are you going to do in five years' time? (ten years' time, next summer, when you leave school/retire, . . .)
– I'm going to ___ .

Robert Markham interviewed the twenty children again at regular intervals. He interviewed them at about 28. The information is in the charts above.

3 Jennifer is talking about her life now. Listen and complete these sentences:
1 She's training to be a doctor because ___ .
2 It takes ___ .
3 She spent ___ .
4 The last seven ___ .
5 She's got a little boy but ___ .
6 Her father ___ .

4 Choose one of the other people above and write a paragraph about him/her now. Begin like this:
___ *wanted to be ___ but/and ___ .*

5 Listen to the tape again. How does the interviewer ask Jennifer:
1 about her job?
2 about the length of training?
3 if it's difficult?
Write the questions down.

6 Write down an occupation, if it is difficult to learn the job or not, and how long it takes. Work in pairs. Use the questions from Exercise 5 to find out about your partner's job, then change partners and tell your new partner about your old one, like this:
Christine said she works in ___ . She had to train ___ .

7 Some occupations need a lot of training. Jennifer says it takes seven or eight years to become a doctor in England. But it's not the same in every country. Look at the table below.

Using the table ask and answer questions about careers:
How long does it take to be a ___ in ___ ?
– It takes ___ .

	primary school teacher	secondary school teacher	doctor	nurse	dentist	policeman/woman
UK	3	4	7/8	3	4/5	varies
USA	4/5	4/5	11–15	2–4	8	varies
Germany	3	4½–5	6	3	5	3
Japan	2	4	4	2/3	4	varies
Brazil	3	4	5	3	4	varies
Spain	3	5	9	3	9	varies
France	4	4–8	7–10	3	5	6 mths
Italy	4	4	6	1–3	5	6 mths

Trevor Simon, son of a diplomat. 'I will probably go to Oxford University. I'm going to own a bank.'

Jennifer Nicholls

MAKE THE MAN?

He asked each of them the question 'What do you want to be when you grow up?' Here are four of the children he interviewed with their answers.

	Trevor	**Jennifer**
Marital status	married	divorced/remarried
Children	0	1
Occupation	stockbroker	hopes to be a doctor
Feels	bored	not very happy
Education	Eton/Oxford	still at university

Now look at the same table and say to your partner:
I'm from ___. I trained for ___ years.
What do I do?
– You're a ___.

8 Many things can influence a decision about a career. Here are some of them. In groups decide which should be most important (****), very important (***), not very important (**), not important at all (*).
Person's/child's choice
Father's/mother's choice
Father's/mother's occupation
What the person/child is good at
Teacher's/school's choice
Rich or poor (can afford a private education)
Where the person lives
Job opportunities

Ask questions around the class, like this:
What is most important?
Do you think the person's choice is very important?
Are the parents' occupations more important than job opportunities?

9 Can you predict their future? Here are two children of ten with information about the way they are today. When they grow up it will be the 21st century. Work in groups to discuss what they will be like and what they are going to do.

James Grant
lives with father
parents divorced
likes science fiction
bad at all school subjects
no brothers or sisters

Jasmin Khan
lives with an aunt in London
likes computers
good at maths and science
not many friends

Decide the children's futures then discuss as a class. Talk about marriage, children, education, occupation, interests.

SUMMARY

Now you can:
make predictions
talk about training and occupation

KEY GRAMMAR
Future tenses
I'm going to be like my mum.
I will probably go to Oxford University.

Take + time
How long does it take to be a doctor?

VOCABULARY
diplomat
primary school
secondary school
sociologist
stockbroker
train (v)
divorced
middle class

2

CLAMPING DOWN ON TOURISTS

It happens to people in London every day. They park in the wrong place and when they come back to their cars, there is a large yellow clamp on the wheel. The car can't be moved until they pay.

1 Listen to this interview with Gina Coppola, an Italian tourist, and answer the questions under the photograph on the next page.
1 What is the object on the car?
2 Why is it there?
3 Who put it there?
4 What must the car owner do now?

2 Now read the letter from Gina below. She is complaining to the Tourist Board.
Gina says the British believe in fair play. This is a stereotype.
Some people believe in fair play and some don't. Which nationalities do you think these common stereotypes of people refer to?

wanting to win	eating good food
the importance of the family	fair play
hard work	saying very little
having a good time	talking a lot
	being friendly

Work in pairs. Ask and answer like this:
I think the British believe in fair play. What do you think?
– Yes I agree/No, I think it's not true. I think ___.
Should a tourist obey the parking rules of a country? Should he or she have special privileges? On the right is a brief look at parking rules in different countries.

3 Look at the signs and text on the right and ask and answer like this:
What can you tell me about parking in the USA?
– In the USA you must/mustn't ___.
If you — you might/could ___ .

4 Now talk about parking and motoring restrictions in your town/country.
In ___ can you park in/on/in front of ___ ?
– Yes you can./No you have to park ___.

1 In the USA you must be very careful where you park – the regulations are very strict in towns.
2 In Britain it is compulsory to wear seat belts in the front of the car, but not in the back. In some countries, for example Germany, it is also compulsory to wear them in the back.
3 In Sweden headlights must be on all the time, even in daylight, which is why you can't turn off the lights on a modern Swedish car while the engine is running.
4 In France the motorway speed limit is 130 kph, in the UK it is 112 kph (70 miles). In Germany there is no legal speed limit, only a recommended one.

5 Make a list of things you *shouldn't* and *mustn't* do when you drive in your country, like this:
dangerous drive too slowly
illegal park on a double yellow line
Now compare with your partner, like this:
I've said that you shouldn't drive too slowly. Have you written that?
– No, I've said that you mustn't park on a double yellow line.

6 Listen to the tape. You will hear two people at the Tourist Board talking about Mrs Coppola's letter (from Exercise 2). Listen once and then write down the reply to her letter as you listen a second time.

Milan 2nd July

Dear Sir,
I have always thought that the British believed in fair play. The British like to be fair. They believe in justice. But why, when I had left my car for only two minutes outside a London department store, did I find a large yellow clamp on the front wheel? This is not fair play! And the expense! It cost me a £19.50 release fee and a ten pound fine! This is ridiculous. I don't think that you should treat a tourist like this.
          Yours very angrily,
          Gina Coppola
P.S. I got a ticket the next day as well and I didn't pay the fine.

7 Group survey.
Gina thought that tourists should have special privileges.
Do you think anyone should have special privileges?
Here is a list of situations. In each case, the traffic warden gave the driver a fine. Do you think he/she was right or not? Work in groups of four. Answer like this:
Yes, I think you should give a ticket to —./No, I don't think you should/ought to give —.

	1	2	3	4
An ambulance waiting outside a shop				
A repair man's car outside a house				
A removal van outside a house				
A tourist in Dover, only ten minutes in the country				
A baker's van outside his shop				
A doctor's car outside a house				

METROPOLITAN POLICE

STOP!
THIS ILLEGALLY PARKED VEHICLE HAS BEEN IMMOBILISED
DO NOT ATTEMPT TO MOVE IT!
IT IS AN OFFENCE TO INTERFERE WITH THE WHEELCLAMP
(MAXIMUM FINE £200 ON CONVICTION)
SEE LABEL ON WINDSCREEN WIPER AS TO RELEASE
IT IS AN OFFENCE TO REMOVE THIS NOTICE
(MAXIMUM FINE £50 ON CONVICTION)

8 Look at the notice on the left and find the word(s) that mean:
1 against the law
2 it's used in the rain
3 the largest possible amount
4 to touch or meddle with
5 a minor crime
6 connected to the major city of a country
7 to try
8 found guilty by a court of law
9 can't be moved

9 Role play
Work in pairs using the information in the label and the boxes below. **A** is a tourist who doesn't understand the label. **B** is a passer-by who tries to explain it. Read the label below and prepare your roles.

METROPOLITAN POLICE
YOUR VEHICLE HAS BEEN IMMOBILISED BY A WHEEL CLAMP*. DO NOT ATTEMPT TO MOVE IT UNTIL YOU HAVE OBTAINED ITS RELEASE. DO THIS:
1. DETACH THIS LABEL AND TAKE IT WITH YOU TO THE POLICE CAR POUND, CUMBERLAND GATE, HYDE PARK, NEAR MARBLE ARCH, LONDON W1, TOGETHER WITH THE FIXED PENALTY NOTICE. A MAP TO HELP YOU FIND THE POLICE CAR POUND IS SHOWN OVERLEAF.
2. A FEE OF £19.50 IS PAYABLE BEFORE THE VEHICLE IS RELEASED. BARCLAYCARD, ACCESS, AMERICAN EXPRESS AND DINERS CLUB CREDIT CARDS, CHEQUES OR CASH, ACCEPTED.
3. IT IS AN OFFENCE TO REMOVE, OR ATTEMPT TO REMOVE THE CLAMP (MAXIMUM FINE ON CONVICTION £200).
4. IF YOU REQUIRE ADVICE ASK A TRAFFIC WARDEN OR POLICE OFFICER.
*(Sections 53-55 Transport Act 1982 refer)
VRM .... POLICE USE ONLY

SUMMARY

Now you can:
talk about parking regulations
give explanations
give opinions

KEY GRAMMAR
Modal verbs
You have to park in a car park.
You mustn't park on a double yellow line.
You shouldn't drive too slowly.

VOCABULARY
clamp   conviction
fair play
fine
justice
offence   payable
privilege   attempt (v)
restriction   complain
ticket   immobilise
traffic warden   interfere

A

Your car has been clamped and you want to know: What do you call the yellow thing on your wheel? Can you take it off? Why or why not? What should you do? Where should you go and how can you get there? What does this mean: "A fee of £19.50 is payable"?

B

A tourist has a clamp on his/her car and he/she doesn't speak English very well. You advise the tourist that he/she has a wheelclamp on the car and he/she mustn't try to take it off because the fine is £200. He/she must take the label to the police. He/she has to pay £19.50 and the police will take it off.

3

1 Is this for me? Thanks, dad.
 – Don't mention it.

2 I'm really very sorry.
 – Oh, never mind.

3 I wonder if you could give me a pound, guv. I'm thirsty.
 – All right. Here you are.

4 I would like to be a doctor or a dentist. What about you?
 – I'd prefer to be a brain surgeon.

5 May I have the name of your insurance company, old chap?
 – Yes, of course.

6 Would you mind if I opened the window a little?
 – Not at all.

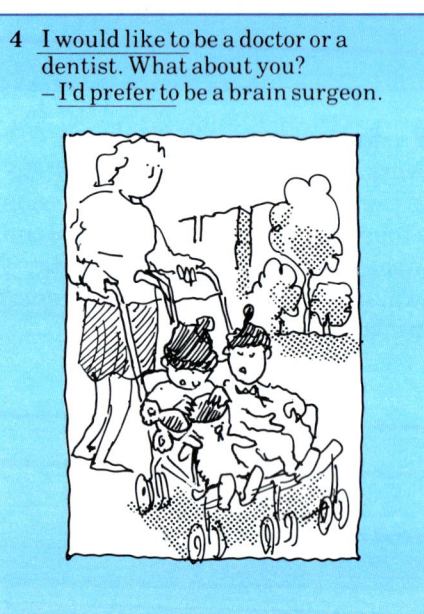

MIND WHAT YOU SAY

Here are some more cartoons from Odile – the French cartoonist who lives in London. These are from her latest book about the British as others see them, *Mind what you say*.

1 Listen to the tape and look at the cartoons. Choose from the functions below to describe what is happening in the underlined phrases: answering thanks asking politely answering an apology showing preference giving advice giving assurance

2 Act out the situations with a partner.

3 Look at these situations. What do you say in each situation? Discuss them with your partner, then write down what you would say.
You step on someone's foot.
You want to borrow something.
You want to change the TV channel.
Someone thanks you for a present you have given them.
Someone asks to borrow your umbrella.
Someone apologises for phoning late at night.
A friend of yours has a terrible cough.
You'd like another cup of tea.
Someone spills your drink and apologises.

4 Work in groups of three. A starts a sentence, B completes it then C responds.
A *Would you mind . . .*
B *Would you mind if I turned the radio off?*
C *Not at all.*

5 Listen to the situations on tape. Some of the replies are wrong. Which ones? Correct them and write them down.

SOCIAL SITUATIONS

7 You'd better stop eating sausages, Mr. Schmidt.
— Do you think so? Why?

8 I'm afraid I may be late. I've got a lot of work in the office.
— Oh, I don't mind. I'm rather busy too.

9 Do you think I could borrow a book?
— Certainly.

10 Would it be possible to go a little slower, Henry?
— I'd rather not.

4

---

6 Act out the correct situations with your partner.

7 Work in pairs. Write two situations on two pieces of paper (like those in Exercise 3). Give them to another pair and ask them to act them out in front of the class.

8 Listen to the sentences on tape and write them down. Then, in pairs, make them into dialogues by writing the sentence which should come before or after.

9 How many ways are there to give advice? Work in groups to find different ways of doing these things. Write as many sentences as possible for each of these headings:
thanking   answering thanks   asking politely   giving advice
showing preference   apologising   answering an apology   giving assurance

SUMMARY

Now you can:
make polite requests
thank
show preference
apologise and respond to apologies
give assurance
give advice

VOCABULARY
cough   assurance
                 brain surgeon
spill   channel (TV)
step   preference

8

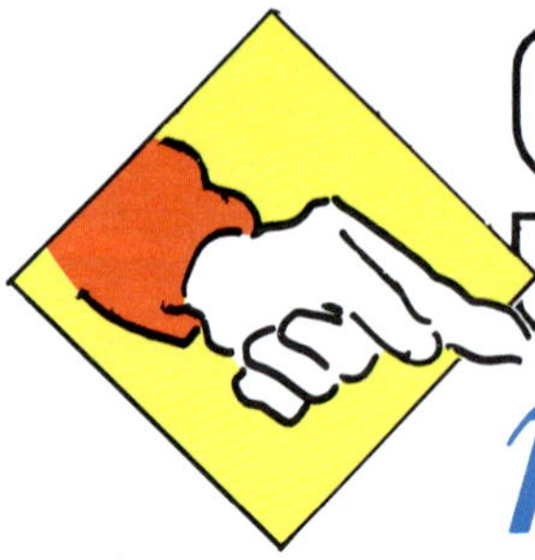

SAY IT WITH *movements*

When you shake your head from one side to the other, what do you mean? Do you mean 'Yes' or do you mean 'No'? If you are American or British you probably mean 'No, I disagree with you', or 'That's not right', but if you are from India, or Bulgaria, for example, then you probably mean the opposite. In India the left to right movement of the head means 'Yes' or 'I understand' or 'That's right'. The body has a language of its own, and all over the world a movement of the hand, a certain look, is one way of communicating information. You can often tell if someone is extremely angry, even if he says nothing at all.

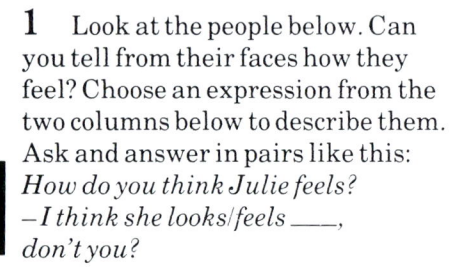

5

1 Look at the people below. Can you tell from their faces how they feel? Choose an expression from the two columns below to describe them. Ask and answer in pairs like this:
How do you think Julie feels?
– I think she looks/feels ___, don't you?

rather	bored
extremely	interested
quite	contented
very	worried
a little	tense
a bit	amused
	shocked
	surprised

We can often tell what a person is thinking or feeling just by watching them. They may not say anything but we know because of some bodily movement or gesture.

2 How do you interpret it when someone does the following? Use *They may/might/could* in your suggestions.
1 Their eyes wander around the room restlessly instead of watching what is going on.
2 They constantly tap their fingers on the table or chair.
3 They keep running their fingers through their hair.
4 They giggle a lot.
5 They don't look at you when they are speaking to you.
6 They stare blankly at you or frown when you speak to them.
7 They keep looking in the mirror.
8 They stand in a corner watching everyone else.

Can you think of any other ways in which people give away their feelings? How do you unintentionally show that you are nervous, for example?
Movements of the hands and face can tell us many things. The picture above shows a group of people at a party. Their faces and movements give a lot of information about how they are feeling. One person dislikes smoking for example. Another person likes dancing. A third person enjoys the company of a friend.

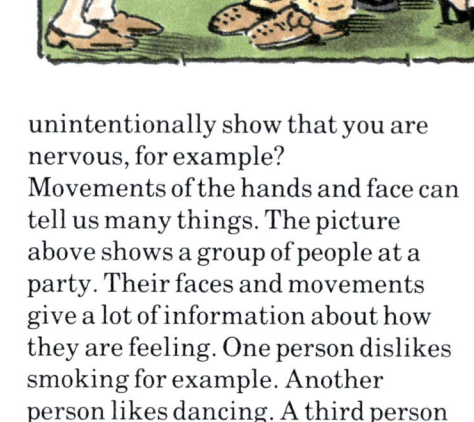

3 Talk about the people like this:
I think that the person on the right/left of the ___ (sitting/standing near/next to, wearing . . .) likes (dislikes, seems, feels, enjoys) ___.
Now talk about them like this:
What can you tell me about the person sitting ___/wearing ___ ?
He's speaking to/listening to/not interested in ___.

Julie   Moira 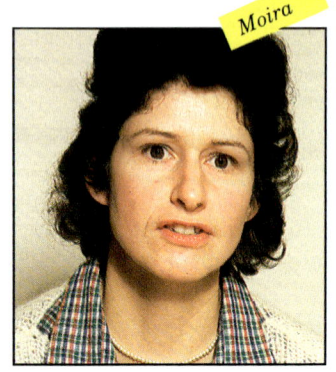   Alan    Charles

9

	A	B
1	driving: Scotland/Germany?	drive on the left/drive on the right
2	eating: Europe/the Far East?	eat with a knife and fork/eat with a spoon and fork or chopsticks
3	drinking tea: UK/many other countries?	add milk/drink it without milk
4	greeting people: Europe/some Far East countries?	shake hands/do not shake hands
5	the use of names: USA/ Germany?	use first names a lot/do not use first names very much
6	the popularity of sheep for food: USA/the Middle East?	mutton and lamb are not eaten/mutton and lamb are very common

4 We have said that a movement of the head is one way of giving information. Work in groups. Try to think of different ways in your country of doing the following.
1 showing you can't hear
2 asking someone to be quiet
3 showing you are tired
4 saying someone is a little crazy
5 asking someone to come closer
6 saying something costs a lot
7 saying someone doesn't like spending money

Ask like this: *Maria, can you tell me one way of ___ in Spain?*
– Yes, like this (she demonstrates).

Some gestures change meaning from country to country. Gesture A below, for example, means 'I am being careful' in France, while in Italy it means 'You be careful'. Its meaning varies from country to country, whereas B is international.

5 What do you think Gesture B means?
Now ask and answer questions using the information in the chart above, like this:
What can you tell me about driving in Scotland compared to in Germany?
– In Scotland you drive on the left, while in Germany you drive on the right.
– In Scotland you drive on the left, whereas in Germany you drive on the right.

6 What would you do if someone came and sat far too close to you, or stood much too close to you at a party? It's a difficult situation. Perhaps there are some of us who wouldn't do anything. But most people would feel uncomfortable. Listen to the tape and answer these questions.
1 How long had the speaker known the man?
2 What was his name?
3 What does she say about how close they were?
4 Were there many people in the room?
5 How did she feel about the situation?

7 Work in pairs. Ask and answer questions like this:
What would you do if you stepped on a man's foot in a bus?
– I think I would apologise/I wouldn't do anything/I would do nothing.
1 You stepped on a man's foot in a bus.
2 Someone stood very close to you in the tube.
3 Someone stood very close to you in an empty room.
4 Someone started to follow you home at night when you were walking.
5 Someone you didn't know kept telephoning you at home.
6 Someone picked up your pen by mistake and put it in his pocket.

SUMMARY

Now you can:

talk about how people look and feel

KEY GRAMMAR
While/whereas
In Scotland you drive on the left, while/whereas in Germany you drive on the right.

Verb and gerund
The man on the left enjoys dancing.

VOCABULARY
communicate   tense
dislike
keep doing   extremely
shake (v)   opposite
              rather
amused   by mistake
contented

CHALMER'S BANK – THE BANK FOR ALL AGES

'CASH IN ON OUR SERVICE'

- Chalmers' money boxes – teach your children to save
- **I'm a Chalmers' first** T-shirt for all first job accounts
- Register at one of our convenient university branches and learn about our student overdraft service (you'll get a free money planner to help you)
- Start a business account and you get an eighteen-carat gold pen
- Travelling abroad? Ask about our complete travel service and free wallet for travellers' cheques and travel documents
- For that new car take out a personal loan and get a free Money Talk diary, with money saving advice
- Near the end of your career? Our special booklet tells you about our financial services for the retired

1 Look at the boxes saying what Chalmers were among the first to do. Make sentences in pairs, like this:
A *Chalmers were among the first to offer . . .*
B *Chalmers were among the first to offer personalised cheques.*

2 Think of some services in your town which have started in the last five years, and what they offer, e.g. restaurant/fast food, bank/cashpoints, petrol stations/self service, dairy/fresh eggs.
Make a list of five points, then ask others in the class:
Which was the first restaurant to offer fast food?
– I think it was ___.

- We were one of the first banks to open
  - on Saturdays
  - at 8.30 a.m.

3 Chalmers' advertisements are very famous. How do you decide what to say in an ad? Listen to John Bertram, who is Public Relations Manager for Chalmers, and complete these sentences, as briefly as possible.

1 The first problem is when ___.
2 He thinks ___ so they suggested introducing ___.
3 The next question is how to ___.
4 His partner suggested giving ___.
5 Another question is ___.
6 ___, for example.
7 ___ is always a problem.
8 Other questions you have to ask about ads are ___.

4 The bank is where you can cash a cheque. Ask your partner where you can do these things:
 buy a ticket for the theatre
 buy a tennis racket
 clean a leather coat

- We were one of the first banks to introduce
  - the cash dispenser
  - the school savings plan
  - the Christmas Club

 send a telex
 make a telephone call
 have English lessons
Think of at least five others, then make dialogues like this:
I don't know where to buy a ticket for the theatre.
– You can buy theatre tickets at a booking agent's.

5 Look at Chalmers' publicity and the list of gimmicks or special services above which Chalmer's Bank offers. Now listen to John Bertram again and tick (✓) the ones he mentions.

Here are some more gimmicks and special services:

>Personalised cheques
>Eurocheques
>Longer opening hours
>Cash dispensers   Drive-in banks
>Leather diaries
>Small business advisers
>Insurance services
>Travel service
>Standing orders   Direct debits

Choose from the words above to complete the sentences below. Then ask and answer in pairs, like this:
What's a cash dispenser?
– It's a machine where you can get money from a bank.
What do you call a machine where you can get money from a bank?
– It's called a cash dispenser.

1 A ____ is a machine where you can get money from a bank.
2 ____ have your name and address printed on them.
3 ____ are who you can talk to about your business problems.
4 ____ is where you can stay in your car and get money.
5 ____ are what you can use to buy things abroad.
6 ____ are where you can write down appointments.
7 The ____ includes advice on visas, foreign currency, insurance and hotel bookings.

6 Work in groups to plan an advertisement for a bank in your town. Decide what services you will offer, what gimmicks you will use (choose from the list above and think of at least one new one). Make suggestions round the group using these phrases:
What about ____?   Why don't we ____?   Let's ____.
Then write a paragraph about your advertisement, starting like this:
We are going to offer/use/introduce ____.

> • We were one of the first banks to offer
>   • introductory savings packs
>   • an advice service for small businesses
>   • personalised cheques

7 Listen to the tape. Mario is cashing a cheque.
Match these questions and the answers below them about the bank clerk.
What does the bank clerk do first?
What does he ask Mario next?
What does he ask then?
What does he ask Mario to do?
What is his last question?

He asks which notes the customer wants.
He asks the amount.
He offers to help.
He asks him to sign the cheque.
He asks about a cheque card.

8 Now work in pairs. Discuss exactly what the bank clerk says, e.g. when he offers to help he says: *Can I help you?*
Listen to the tape. Were you right? Mario asks three questions. What are they?

9 Your partner wants to cash a cheque in a British bank. Give him advice by completing the sentences below:
First the teller offers to help. What does he say?
– He probably says '____'.
Then you say 'Can you ____?'
Then he asks '____?'
In England they can't ____.
You will have to have ____.

10 Listen to the tape. You will hear someone explaining how to complete the cheque below. As you listen, complete the cheque.

SUMMARY

Now you can:
talk about bank services
write out a cheque in an English bank
make suggestions

KEY GRAMMAR
Infinitive phrases
We were one of the first banks to offer personalised cheques.

Suggestions
Let's introduce the name of the bank to children.

Defining relatives
A cash dispenser is a machine where you can get money from a bank.

VOCABULARY
account	gimmick
amount	overdraft
cash dispenser	public relations
document	register (v)

11 Make out a blank cheque. Now give instructions to your partner to complete the cheque.

6

BECOMING A WOMAN IN JAPAN

日本の女

Many people still think that the Japanese woman is one of the least liberated in the world. They think of the Japanese woman who wears a kimono down to her ankles and walks behind her husband, or of the geisha who looks after a man's every need. But women's liberation has reached Japan too, and things are changing. On the other hand, women in some European countries are less liberated than we realise. Women in one Swiss canton, for example, do not have the vote.

Momoko Watson (Mo for short) is a 29-year-old woman who comes from a Tokyo suburb. She is the daughter of a professor of engineering at Tokyo University and her mother teaches at a school of dress design. But Mo lives in a small town outside of London and, as her surname suggests, she is married to an Englishman. How typical is she?

7

1 Read the text above and write a summary in your own words, beginning with the prompts below.
Many people think that Japanese women ____.
But things are ____.
On the other hand, in some ____.
Mo Watson is ____.
But she lives ____.

2 Listen to Momoko talking about her life and complete these sentences about her.
1 I had ____.
2 I studied ____.
3 I got a job as ____.
4 In 1980 ____.
5 I was still ____.
6 My parents ____.
7 Now I ____.

3 Look at the sentences you have written. Do you think it is common or unusual for a Japanese woman to do these things? Discuss each sentence in pairs.

Now compare your decisions with other members of the class, like this:
We think that studying English at university might be quite common among Japanese women.
– We agree./We don't agree. We think it's probably quite unusual.

4 Now listen to an interviewer asking Mo some questions. Were your decisions in Exercise 3 correct? Ask and answer in pairs:
What did Mo say about studying English?
– She said it was quite common.
What did you say about it?
– I also said it was quite common./I said I thought it was unusual.

In Japan both men and women go to university and both men and women study arts subjects such as English. But very few women study science, medicine or engineering. In engineering classes of thirty or forty students, there may be only one or two women. Men and women both go to university in order to get good jobs: men want to work for a big company, be successful, earn a lot of money and support a family; women, on the other hand, want to work for a big company because they have a better chance of meeting a successful man and getting married. This is changing, however, and Japanese women are beginning to think about themselves. They are beginning to look for a job because they like it rather than because they hope to find a good husband.

Men have a job for the whole of their lives and usually stay with the same company. A woman may work for up to ten years, but after that she usually marries. Most women are married by the age of 27, then they stay at home and look after the children. A man might not mind if his wife goes to work, but she must look after everything in the house as well. A man does not cook or look after the children. When he comes home, his meal must be ready. The woman may go out in the afternoon, shopping with her friends or just to have a chat, but she must be home by four o'clock to prepare the meal. Then she may have to wait a long time for her man to come home. Often he has to go out for a drink after work: if he doesn't he may not rise very high in the company. The man often does not come home until eleven o'clock or later. After her children are grown up, a woman can go back to work, but it is not easy. If her old company takes older women back, she might be lucky. But most women find it difficult to get a good job when they are older.

5 Read the second passage about Japan and complete the chart as in the examples.

	Men	Women	Both
*study subjects like English			
*study engineering			
*go to university to get good jobs			
go to university because they want a good husband			
go to university because they want to be successful			
*work for a lifetime			
work for five to ten years			
get married by 27			
*cook the meals			
*look after the house			
*look after the children			
come home after 11 o'clock			
come home by 4 o'clock			

Now write sentences about the chart, like this:
Both men and women study subjects like English.
Only men study engineering.

Ask and answer questions about the chart, like this:
Who is used to working for a lifetime in Japan?
– Only men are used to working for a lifetime.

6 Make a similar chart for your country, using the starred (*) items from the chart above, and others of your own, and complete it in groups. Ask questions like this:
Who is used to cooking the meals?
Does everyone agree?

7 Ask and answer questions about men and women in other countries, like this:
In what country/part of the world are women/men used to wearing jeans?
– Both men and women are used to wearing jeans in the West.

Use these prompts (and others): driving   having a good education
wearing jeans   working   voting   staying at home
covering their faces   joining/fighting in the army   going out to pubs
playing sports   having arranged marriages   marrying very young

8 Mo is a career woman and not a housewife. Look at the definitions and the single words below. Now combine words on the left with those on the right, like the example, to answer the definitions below.

crafts   worker
office   wife
family   man
career   girl
school   woman
house   bride
sports   *person
war
sales
business
factory

* Many people in English-speaking countries prefer to use the word *person* in place of *man/woman*, for example *salesperson* (rather than *salesman/woman*).

1 ____ = a man or woman who sells for a company
2 ____ = a man who is a good husband and father
3 ____ = a woman with a good professional job
4 ____ = a young woman who is still at school
5 ____ = a man/woman who is good at sports
6 ____ = a woman who married a soldier in World War 2
7 ____ = a man or woman who owns a company
8 ____ = a man or woman who makes things by hand such as pottery or textiles
9 ____ = a woman who doesn't go out to work
10 ____ = a man or woman who works in a factory
11 ____ = a man or woman who works in an office

9 Look at the advertisement below. When it appeared in London the slogan was written on it. Work in two equal groups to prepare arguments for and against the advertisement. Then divide into pairs, one person from each group. One person is the advertising agent who devised the advert; the other is a member of a Women's Group. Act out the conversation you would have about the advertisement.

SUMMARY

Now you can:
talk about habit and custom

KEY GRAMMAR
Gerund (as noun)
Studying English is quite common.

Used to + ing
Only men are used to working for a lifetime.
Who is used to cooking the meals?

Both/only
Both men and women study subjects like English.
Only men study engineering.

VOCABULARY
geisha   liberation
kimono
              look after
liberated   short for

FIND A NEW YOU AT THE SLIM INN

FIND A NEW YOU

Pat Laurence describes a day at the Slim Inn.

'I hadn't been very happy for months. I was too fat and I felt like a change. I had been told by my doctor that I had to lose weight and I had been put on a very strict diet. It was boring and it hadn't worked. So I went to the Slim Inn. I'll never forget the first day. After we had been woken up by music we all got up, put on our Slim Inn jogging suits and went for a run. Then we all came back for a swim, and a shower. After I had been weighed for the first time, I got dressed and we were given our first 250 calorie breakfast. It was delicious: a poached egg on freshly baked granary toast, melon with grapes and yoghurt. Then we all went to the garden for an hour: we had all been given a choice of activities so after breakfast I sat down and planned my day.

1 Listen to the tape and complete the paragraph below:

🟨 *Who is it for?*
You should come to the Slim Inn if you are ____ or feel like ____.

🟨 *What can you do?*
You can ____ and ____.

🟨 *What can the Slim Inn offer you?*
The Slim Inn has ____ and ____ and it's the only ____.

🟨 *What do you get?*
You get a ____ with ____ and lots of ____.

🟨 *How do I find out more?*
Ring ____ or write to ____.

2 The Slim Inn has a friendly atmosphere. Here are some other words which can be used to describe the atmosphere of a place:
bad good happy calm congenial exciting romantic cold warm unfriendly healthy unhealthy
Discuss what the words mean in groups.
Make a list of places you know and write one or two adjectives next to them. Now talk to your partner like this:
I never go to Ronnie's. It's got a very cold and unfriendly atmosphere.
– I've never been there, but I like Mario's. It's got a very romantic atmosphere.

3 Read what Pat Laurence said about the Slim Inn and complete these sentences about her first day:
1 After she ____, she went jogging.
2 After she ____, she got dressed.
3 After she ____, she went to the garden.
4 After she ____, she planned her day.

4 Work in pairs. Here is a list of events in the lives of two of Pat Laurence's friends. However, the lists are not complete. Complete them in your own words (one person does one list only), and then ask and answer questions like this:
What had happened to Jane Dunn before she was sixteen?
– She had taken all her school exams.

	Jane Dunn	Sue Burton
16	taken all her school exams	
18		got married
20	finished university	
25		had a baby
30		
35		
40		

5 How do you feel if you have been doing the same things for weeks? You feel like a change! Look at these situations and match Column **A** with Column **B**.

A You have just been	B and you feel like
told some bad news	a long rest
woken up	a day by the sea
brought home from hospital	leaving your job
given the day off	staying in on your own
given first prize in the lottery	a celebration
given the sack	a party
given your exam results	going back to bed
given too much work to do	a drink

Work in pairs. Tell your partner about three things that have happened:
I've just been given the sack and I feel like a drink. I've ____.
Now change partners and ask your new partner:
What did he tell you?   *– He told me he'd been ____.*
What's he going to do?   *– He's going to have ____.*

8

15

WE TAKE GOOD CARE OF YOU

take you jogging ☐ help you plan your diet ☐ teach you about good eating habits ☐ lead you in group discussions ☐ show you health and fitness videos ☐ give you health tutorials ☐ give you tennis lessons ☐ relax you in sauna and jacuzzi sessions ☐ weigh you every morning ☐ teach you yoga and relaxation techniques ☐ instruct you in swimnastics ☐ instruct you in aerobics ☐

6 Look at the list of activities available and use them to complete your timetable below:

6.30	wake up	12.00	
7.00		13.00	lunch
7.45		14.00	
8.30	breakfast	16.00	
9.00	rest and relaxation in the lounge/garden	17.00	rest
		18.00	dinner
10.00		19.30	
11.00		21.30	
		22.30	bed

Write a description of your timetable like this:
First I was woken up by ____. After I'd had breakfast/been taken jogging I was instructed in ____. Next/after that ____.
Now read your description to your partner while he/she takes notes. Change partners and, using your notes, describe what your first partner said, like this:
She said that after she had been given breakfast, she ____.
Now work in pairs to discuss tomorrow's timetable:
What will you be doing after lunch/at 10.00 a.m. tomorrow? – I think I'll be jogging/watching videos/in a tutorial.
At the Slim Inn Pat was given a living pattern chart. Before that she had never been shown why she was overweight. This is what she discovered.

7 Listen to the tape and complete the chart for Pat:

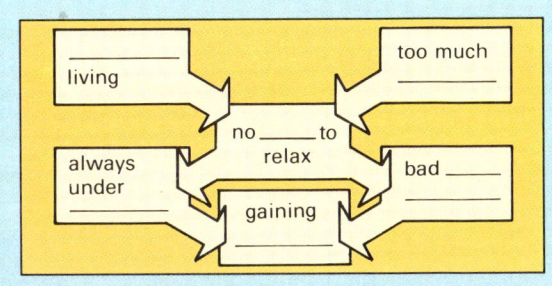

[Chart: living ____, too much ____, no ____ to relax, always under ____, bad ____, gaining ____]

Now complete this paragraph:
Gaining weight is often caused by ____ and ____.
These are often the results of having no ____, which in itself comes from ____ and ____.
What would you advise Pat to do?

SUMMARY

Now you can:

give more varied descriptions of places and feelings

KEY GRAMMAR
Past perfect passive
We had all been given a choice of activities.

Future continuous
What will you be doing tomorrow at . . .?
I'll be jogging.

Reported speech
He told me he'd been given the day off.

VOCABULARY

atmosphere	cause
calories	tone up
fitness	calm
jacuzzi	
meditation	congenial
muscles	overweight
swimnastics	romantic
sauna	strict

8 Listen again. Find two sentences beginning with *when* and write them down. Now find two sentences starting with another word which has a similar meaning to *when*. What is the word? Listen to Pat's last speech and write the sentence starting with *if*. Why is it different from the other two which start with *if*?

9 Choose from one of these ideas or your own ideas for a special week/weekend and plan the activities in groups:
week of sport   a wholefood week
a gourmet weekend   a farm week
a camping weekend
a meditation and yoga week
Make suggestions like this:
No one/nobody likes/enjoys ____ but I think everyone/everybody might like ____.
Take notes and write a paragraph about the week you have planned.

8

16

EURO CHICK

Most people have heard about the European Common Market. There is a European Parliament in Strasbourg, for example. What does it do? There is also a Court of Justice in Luxembourg. What does that do? The truth is that most people don't know. In fact, the decisions of the Common Market administration affect the lives of people throughout the community. They affect the price of lamb, for example. They affect how much money will be given to support a particular country. And they affect chickens.

One matter which is being discussed at the moment is the future of more than 250 million battery chickens which lay most of the eggs for the 315 million inhabitants of the community. A battery chicken has a miserable life, lived in a space of 400 cubic centimetres – no bigger than a large piece of paper. Now, if the authorities in the community are successful, the Common Market battery chicken is going to be a much happier bird altogether, because laws will be passed to make sure that they all have 450 cu. cm, or even 500 cu. cm. space. However, nothing happens in a day, and it may take seven or eight years for the change to be made. Meanwhile, the chickens will have to wait. That's bad news for the 80 to 95% of chickens which live in batteries in most European countries, not quite such bad news in France, where just 64% of chickens live in batteries, and hardly important at all in Greece where 87% of the chicken population run around completely free. Not important, that is, unless you're a Greek chicken living, sleeping, clucking, and laying eggs in a miserable 400 cubic centimetres.

1 Complete the following notes from the text:
1 Most people don't know anything ____.
2 The things which Common Market decisions affect include ____.
3 There are nearly as many ____.
4 Battery chickens live ____.
5 In most European countries ____.

2 Find words in the text which mean:
a group of people living or working together
help financially
problem, issue
during this time
not very
make a noise like a chicken

3 Often, when you want something done, it can take a long time. The chickens will have to wait several years for the change to be made. Here are some other situations:
Your car needs repairing.
Your teeth need filling.
Your clothes need cleaning.
Your hair needs cutting.
Your coat needs mending.
In pairs, discuss who does these things (e.g. a mechanic) and list some more situations.

Now do this quiz in groups. Ask and answer questions like this:
If you go to this person it shouldn't take long for your car to be repaired. Who is it?
– *It's a mechanic.*

4 In the European Common Market there are always several matters which are being discussed. Think of some matters in your country which are being discussed and talk about them, like this:
At the moment ____ is being discussed/talked about in ____. My opinion is that ____./I think that ____. What do you think?

5 There are several main bodies which look after the business of the Common Market.
Listen to the tape and complete these sentences:
These Commissioners ____.
The Parliament decides ____.
The Council of Ministers takes ____.

Now complete these boxes:

The Commission	The Parliament
Number of Commissioners	Location
Number from Germany	Number of members
Number from Luxembourg	Can decide about

The Council of Ministers	The Court of Justice
Number of members	Makes decisions about

6 Group work. Discuss the topics below in groups of two or three. If you were able to make a proposal for a new law in your country, what would you choose? Decide on a proposal.
Present the proposal to Group B. Group B discusses the proposal, and then reports to the class, like this:
Group A gave us a proposal about ___. We have been discussing whether to agree with it or not, and we think ___.

7 Here are two problems. Think about them in your groups and act out your discussions.
1 Parking: There is not enough space in your town. Are you going to build multi-storey car parks in the centre, or on the outskirts?
2 Your town has enough money for a new sports stadium or a new library, but not both.
Group A – discuss a solution to 1.
Group B – discuss a solution to 2.

Now approach the other group and present your proposals, like this:
We have (problem) and we have to decide whether to ___ or ___; and we weren't sure whether to ___ or ___ / we didn't know whether to ___ or ___.
We discussed the matter and decided ___. The reasons for this are ___. What do you think?

8 Imagine that you have been elected to serve as a Euro MP for your country/a European country. In pairs, list the changes you intend to make, like this:
I'll make a European passport.
Use these ideas: travel trade laws justice

Now work in groups and ask and answer like this:
What did you say about travel?
– We said we would make a European passport.

9 Work in groups to do this quiz. Can you match the populations in Column **A** with the correct answer in Column **B**? Ask and answer like this:
Have you any idea about the population of ___?
– Yes, I think it is about ___.
Does anyone disagree?
– Yes, I do. I think it's ___.

A	B
230 million	Japan
315 million	the European Common Market
117 million	the Soviet Union
267 million	the United States

Here are the dates when countries joined the Common Market. Match the columns, then ask and answer questions, like this:
Can you tell me when ___ joined the Common Market?
Do you know one of the first/last countries to join?

A	B
18 April 1951	Greece the Irish Republic Spain
1 January 1973	West Germany France Portugal
1 January 1981	Belgium the Netherlands Luxembourg
1 January 1986	Denmark Great Britain Italy

10 Listen to the tape and take notes. You will hear someone talking about the objectives of the Common Market. Take notes about each of the following objectives.
Free Trade   Freedom to work
Agriculture   Financial support

Now compare notes and talk like this:
Robert, what did the speaker say about free trade?
– He said that ___. He added that ___. He mentioned that ___.

11 Here are some other communities in the world:
MAGHREB (e.g. Morocco, Tunisia)
ASEAN (e.g. Indonesia, Thailand)
COMECON (e.g. Poland, Vietnam)
What do you think are their concerns and interests? Build up a list in groups for each community. Use phrases like these:
What do you think ___ might be/ought to be doing?
– We think that in ___ they will be/might be could be/should be concerned about ___.
Compare your results.

SUMMARY
Now you can:
discuss proposals

KEY GRAMMAR
Passive + infinitive
...it may take seven or eight years for the change to be made.

Present continuous passive
One matter which is being discussed at the moment...

Indirect questions
We have been discussing whether to agree to it or not.

VOCABULARY
administration
authorities
battery chicken
budget
commissioner
concerns (n)
council
inhabitant
judge (n)
objective (n)
policy
proposal

region
seat
work permit
cluck
develop
lay eggs
pass (a law)
put forward
support
miserable

9

18

THE INSIDE STORY NEWSPAPER

Phil Osborne – Night Editor of the Guardian

NEWSPAPERS: HOW OBJECTIVE ARE THEY?

Newspapers are one of the main sources from which we learn what is going on – in world politics, science, local government, the arts, fashion, food, education and sport. The papers we choose show our interests and usually the politics which we believe in. There are nine national daily newspapers in Britain, of which five are tabloids and four are quality papers. Do these newspapers really serve the people they are written for? Many people question the objectivity of newspapers. How objective are they? We might be better able to judge if we understand how a newspaper is produced. Reporters, of course, are the source from which the facts must come, but there are many other people involved in and influencing a newspaper.

1 Match these words from the text with the definitions on the right:

tabloid	where something comes from
objective	have an effect on
judge	without expressing opinion
reporters	small, often low-quality newspaper
source	decide what is good or bad
influence	people who find out about events

2 The chart on the right shows the organisation of a major newspaper. Listen to the tape and complete it.

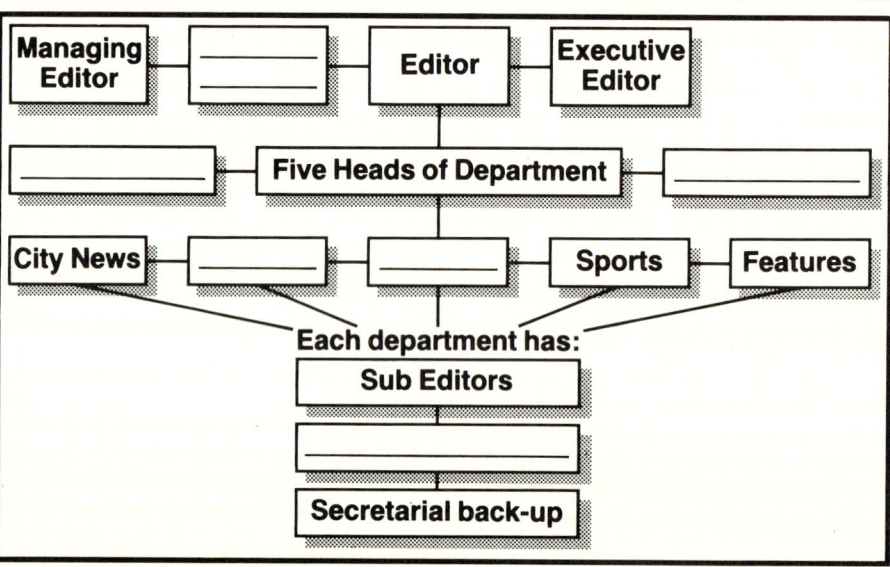

Managing Editor — ___ — Editor — Executive Editor
___ — Five Heads of Department — ___
City News — ___ — ___ — Sports — Features
Each department has:
Sub Editors
___
Secretarial back-up

There are several conferences during each working day in which news stories are discussed. The paper is printed by 9.40 each evening after which it is ready for distribution. This is a typical day's timetable:

10.00 am	Reporters/editors/department heads arrive
10.00 – 11.00	Mail is read News list is prepared Stories are given to journalists in each department First reaction to early news
11.15 – 11.45	First editorial conference is held with editors and department heads (ideas, possibilities are discussed)
11.45 – 1.00 pm	Department heads return to desks Conference is held by the Editor with leader writers, journalists and specialists
1.00 – 2.30	Lunch, during which journalists often do a lot of work
2.30 – 4.15	Meeting with Night Editor, who starts his day here and is now given information about the morning's events
3.00 – 3.15	Space conference where position of advertisements/amount of space for each section is discussed The paper is put together; articles are written
	Some early pages are printed now
6.15 – 6.25	A final conference; more detailed than the first. The importance of the different stories is discussed
8.40	Page one, which is the last page, is sent to the printer by this time
9.40	The paper is now printed in its first edition
11.00	Second edition
12.30 am	Third edition
2.00	Fourth edition

3 Look at the timetable and answer these questions:

1. When is space discussed?
2. When is the final conference held?
3. When is the second edition printed?
4. When is the paper put together?
5. When are the articles written?
6. When is the newspaper ready for distribution?

4 Ask questions and answer them from the chart below, like this:

What happens | at 11.15?
              | from 11.15 to 11.45?

– At 11.15 there is the first editorial conference, in which new ideas are discussed.

At ___	there is	the first editorial conference	in which . . .
From ___ to ___		lunch	during which . . .
		a conference with the leader writers	after which . . .
		a space conference	
		a meeting with the Night Editor	
		a final conference	

5 Ask and answer questions in pairs, like this:
What's the name of the person by whom the newspaper (front page, leader column . . .) is printed (edited, written . . .)?
– *He's called the ___ .*

6 In groups make questions from the chart below, and answer them. Then ask other groups about their answers, like this:
What's the name of the person from whom you can buy a newspaper? or *What's the name of the person you can buy a newspaper from?*

person/people		you can buy a newspaper
country	which	you can read *La Stampa*
short sentence		you can read about an item of news
text	whom	you can understand the summary of a story in a newspaper
department		the paper is written
		the paper is printed
		deals with financial matters

7 HOW DO YOU CHOOSE YOUR NEWSPAPER?

Discuss like this:
I like a newspaper which is/has
- a good sports section
- good political columnists
- an amusing cartoonist
- few advertisements
- cheap
- easy to read on a bus/train
- a good international section
- good crosswords
- not too right/left wing

Now ask and answer:
Is there anything else? What about ___ ?
– *Yes, I like that too./No, that's not very important for me.*

8 Here are some qualities a good journalist might have. Rank them 1 (most important) to 7 (least important). Do the other students agree with you?
curiosity   honesty   extrovert personality
ability to work hard   self-discipline
good command of langue

9 Here are some headlines from a newspaper. Ask and answer like this:
I think Headline 2 probably comes from the city section. Do you agree?
– *Yes, I do./No, I think it might come from ___ .*

(1) New Japanese computer worries Americans

(2) FRENCH LEFT CONTROL CITY

(3) LAST-MINUTE GOAL HELPS SPAIN

(4) Dollar up and up and up

(5) Prime Minister to Russia

10 Match the headlines with the sentences below and write sentences about each headline, like this:
This will be an article in which I will read about a football match between Spain and another country/from which I will learn about ___ .

a   At the end of her three-day visit Mrs Thatcher is expected to visit the . . .
b   Real Madrid drew with Liverpool in a spectacular match last night.
c   After the surprise result in the Paris elections last night, we asked people . . .
d   The Mishumati 3000 will sell at under £1,500, nearly £200 lower than its closest competitor.
e   . . . rose by 10 cents on the Financial Times Index last night . . .

11 Write about the cartoon below. What sort of newspaper does it come from? What is it about? What is the caption? Where does it appear in the newspaper?

SUMMARY

Now you can:
make priorities
discuss timetables

KEY GRAMMAR
Relatives + preposition
There is a conference in which ideas are discussed.

Present simple passive
When is the paper put together?

VOCABULARY
conference	source
deputy	tabloid
distribution	distribute
editor	edit
journalist	influence (v)
objectivity	involve
quality paper	judge
reporter	print

MEDIA

10

20

Television

If someone tells you 'You have to watch the news on Channel Four and the play on Channel Two this evening', will you do it? You probably think that you have the right to choose the programmes that you like. But how much choice do we really have? Do television channels really show the things that you want to see? Or do you sometimes watch things on TV that you would never watch on film or in the theatre? On commercial television in Britain advertising and programmes are completely separate. Because of non-commercial stations the British public are used to programmes that the government and advertisers cannot influence. In America it is usually the opposite – the advertisers pay for the programmes.

1 Read the text and listen to the tape. You will hear part of the same text but a word is left out four times. What is the word?
What other word can be used in its place?

2 Complete the table below and then ask and answer in pairs, using these questions:
How many hours a week do you watch sport programmes (news, music, comedy, . . .)?
What percentage is that of your total viewing hours?

Type of programme	Hours per week	Percentage of total
News		
Documentaries		
Soap operas		
Comedies		
Dramas		
Music		
Chat shows		
Sports		
Films		
Total		

3 Make a class top ten of TV programmes using programmes/programme categories from your own country. Each student makes a statement to the person next to him/her like this:
____ *is the programme that I like best. What about you?*
Take notes and then discuss as a class.

4 Look at the types of programmes in Exercise 2. Choose the type you like most/least and ask and answer in pairs.
Which type of programme do you like best?
– Documentaries are the programmes that I like best.
Which is your favourite documentary?
– I think it's probably ____.

Imagine that you are locked in a room for one month and can only watch one programme. What will it be? Explain your choice to your partner.?
Now write a short paragraph about your partner and read it to the class.

5 Compare your opinions with others in the class, like this:
Do you think there should be more/less sport (news, music, . . .) on TV?
– Yes, I do./No, I don't, but I think ____.

> Only one third of households in the UK own their televisions. Two thirds rent televisions and because of this the teletext service is growing more rapidly in the UK than in any other country. Teletext is an information service that is operated by the TV channels. In the UK the BBC operates CEEFAX and ITV operates ORACLE.

In 1983–84, 10,388 advertising scripts were sent to the Independent Broadcasting Authority for approval, of which:

9,221 were general
215 were medical
512 were semi-medical
440 were financial

There are certain products or services which cannot be advertised on British television. These include fortune tellers, computer dating services, undertakers, betting shops, cigarettes and cigarette tobacco, private detectives, contact lenses, smoking cures and baldness clinics.
Certain products can't be advertised before or after children's programmes, including alcohol, liqueur chocolates, cigars, tobacco and matches. Other products such as medicines for children can only be advertised after 9 p.m. when most small children are in bed.

6 In groups, talk about what products should and should not be advertised on television, and the restrictions which control them. Complete the chart below and ask others in your group about their charts, like this:
Sleeping tablets are one of the things that I think shouldn't be advertised/should be unrestricted/should be shown only after 9 p.m. What do you think?

	Not at all	Restricted times	Unrestricted
sleeping tablets			
cigarettes			
cigars			
beer			
spirits			
wine			
sports cars			
nose sprays			
chocolate			
butter			
butchers			
X-rated films			
toys			

7 Listen to the tape and complete the chart below about television in Europe.

	Number of channels			
	1	2	3	4	Total
Countries with commercial stations				X	
Countries with non-commercial stations			X		

8 What did you watch last night? What do you learn from television?
Write a short paragraph, like this:
I watched ___ and ___, both/all of which were excellent (very good, dreadful, . . .), one/two of which were ___. I also watched ___ from which I learnt about ___.
Or write a short paragraph and describe an interesting or funny plot.
Begin like this:
Last night I saw ___ in which a man ___.

In Britain commercial television can have a maximum of six minutes of advertising per hour on average. Advertisements may occur at the beginning or end of a programme and in breaks in the middle. These must be breaks that occur naturally, such as a change of scene in a drama, a change of players in a game show or between acts or guests in a variety or chat show. No advertising can interrupt the following: half-hour documentary programmes for schools, religious services, half-hour children's programmes, royal ceremonies, parliamentary broadcasts or any programme that's less than twenty minutes long.

9 The map below shows the number of advertising minutes per day in thirteen European countries. Look at the map and in pairs ask questions like this:
In which country is the most/least advertising allowed? Where is the advertising restricted to 60 (20, 40, . . .) minutes?

Advertising in Europe

20 Available advertising minutes per day

Norway
Finland 25
Sweden
Holland 30
Ireland 83
Britain 140
Denmark
Belgium
W. Germany 40
Lux. 68
France 54
Austria 20
Portugal 135
Spain 99
Italy 65
Switzerland 60
Greece 110

SUMMARY

Now you can:
talk about television viewing
talk about favourites

KEY GRAMMAR
Relative *that* (and deleted *that*)
Do television channels really show the things (that) you want to see?

Relative *which* and preposition
I saw two programmes, both of which were excellent.

VOCABULARY
channel	programme	variety
chat show	script	commercial
documentary	soap opera	non-commercial
information service	teletext	

MEDIA

11

22

UNLOCKING A LEGEND
The Story of Charlie Chaplin

These are the symbols of a man who was and is the world's most famous film comedian. Even after his death the legend lives on. Charlie Chaplin's little tramp is still the symbol of the 'little' man, who experiences all of the difficulties and sadness of life, but who is never discouraged.

Chaplin is a hero to many people, including David Robinson, film critic of *The Times*, although he hardly ever had any contact with him when the comedian was alive. Although he saw Chaplin five times, he only talked to him on three of those occasions. How did he feel when he had the chance to see documents about Chaplin's life which no outsider had seen before? After Oona, Chaplin's wife, said that Robinson could write a biography with her help, he still had moments of doubt. He thought there were already too many books about Chaplin. Did the world want another? However, in the cellar of the Manoir de Ban, the Chaplins' Swiss mansion, he found a real treasure: scrapbooks, studio records and more. Treasure followed treasure: posters and programmes, photographs and snapshots. A biographer rarely has such a great opportunity.

1 Can you find words in the text which mean the following:
a funny man/woman
a person with no home and no possessions
to lose hope
someone whom people admire
not often
opportunity

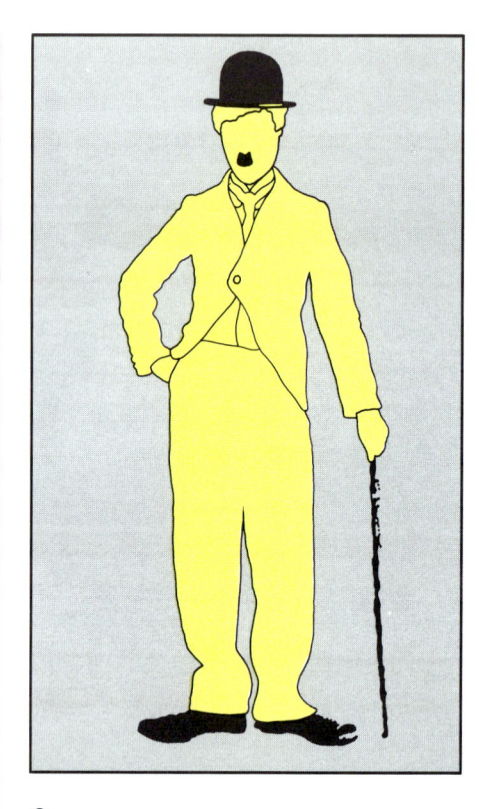

2 There are several occupations mentioned in the text. How many can you find?

3 Complete these sentences about the text.
1 Even after his death, Chaplin is still ____.
2 To many people, Chaplin represents ____.
3 David Robinson hardly ____.
4 He was the first person to ____.
5 In Manoir de Ban he found ____.

4 Ask and answer questions about your favourite stars like this:
Charlie Chaplin is my favourite comedian. Do you like him?
– *Yes, I do. I like his films very much. (My favourite film is ____.)*
– *I hardly remember/know him.*
Talk about comedians, musicians, film directors, painters, actors etc.

5 In the UK in 1983 only 50 million people bought cinema tickets, while a few years earlier more than 200 million tickets were sold. Most British people hardly ever go to the cinema. What about you?
Ask and answer questions, like this:
How often do you go to the cinema? (theatre, opera, concerts, ...)
– *I hardly ever/frequently/don't often/rarely go to ____.*

Chaplin had many famous leading ladies, including Georgia Hale and Virginia Cherrill, but not all of them were fond of him off the screen. Virginia Cherrill, the gentle, blind flower girl from *City Lights*, told Robinson that she and Charlie had never really liked each other at all.

6 Listen to the actress talking on the tape and write down the sentences which contain these words: he told me to
he told me not to   he asked me to
he said to me that I shouldn't
he said that I couldn't
What does she say she's doing tomorrow? List your plans for next week and ask and answer in pairs:
What are you doing on ____?
– *I'm playing tennis with ____.*

7 Ask your partner to give you a command and then do what he/she tells you. Let the class guess what he/she has said, like this: *I think he asked you to look at the ceiling.*
Use these words: asked/told you to

8 Listen to the tape. An English director is on the set of a film about a 19th century English town.

MEDIA

You will hear several requests and commands. Write them down and change them, like this:
Arthur, don't put the lamp there.
He told Arthur not to put the lamp there.

9 The director asks Anne to speak more quickly. He asks her *if* she could speak more quickly.
Write down three requests (e.g. *Could you lend me your pen/open the window?*), then ask and answer in groups of three, like this:
A (to B) *Could you lend me your pen?*
C (to B) *What did he ask you?*
B (to C) *He asked me if I could lend him my pen.*

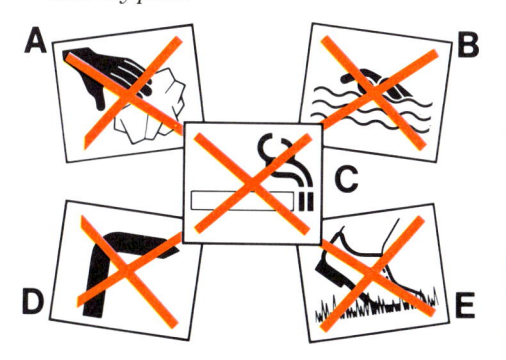

A	B
'He complains when I'm late.'	Try to relax
'I can rarely make myself cry.'	Have voice lessons
'She can't remember her lines.'	Put her on a diet
'I frequently lose my voice in front of the cameras.'	Use onions
'I can't help arguing with her.'	Drink honey and lemon
'How can I make her lose weight?'	Use cue cards
'He says I don't speak clearly enough.'	Get up earlier
'She's hardly ever on time.'	Arrange to phone her in the morning

11 In Column **A** above there are eight statements, made by a film director and an actress. In Column **B** there is advice for the actress/director. First, match the problems and the advice, then decide who said each statement (actress or director).
Now work in groups of three. A is the actress, B is the director and C is the film producer. Make dialogues using the prompts above, like this:
A *He complains when I'm late.*
C *Well, why don't you get up earlier?*
B *She's hardly ever on time!*
C *You could always arrange to phone her in the morning.*

10 What do these signs tell you? Ask and answer in pairs, like this:
What does ___ mean?
– It means that you shouldn't/mustn't/can't smoke.

Now look at the signs and make sentences like this:
He/she pointed at the sign and asked/told me to/not to ___. Where was I?
– I think you were on the street.

SUMMARY

Now you can:
express likes and dislikes
talk about frequency
give advice

KEY GRAMMAR
Adverbs of frequency
I hardly remember him.
They rarely go to the cinema.

Indirect commands
First he told me to be in London on Monday.
He asked me if I could lend him my pen.

VOCABULARY
biography
comedian
critic
hero
legend
outsider
screen
symbol
tramp
treasure
represent

12

SEEING IS

Several years ago a British author and TV presenter, John Berger, presented a TV series called *Ways of Seeing*, and this series was later published as a book, with the same title. In his series Berger examined the importance of pictures and symbols, and how they affect our view of the world. Quite a lot of the series looked at advertising and at how advertisers use the visual world to sell their products.

To begin with, let's have a look at advertising campaigns. Some advertising campaigns have been so successful that it is no longer necessary to give the name of the product – the symbol is enough to make you think of it. Take this symbol for example: Although there is no name, everyone knows it means Mercedes Benz. The symbol is so famous that people recognise it.

1 Work in groups. Look at these symbols and ask each other questions.
*Do you know what **a** is?*
– Yes, I recognise it. I think it's the symbol for ____.
– Although I don't recognise it, I think it might be for ____.
*What does **c** make you think of? – It makes me think of ____.*

2 Now write three sentences, like this:
The silver lady is so famous that most people know it is the symbol for ____.

3 Advertisements take many forms, some of which are in Column **A**. In Column **B** there are some opinions of these forms of advertising. Match the opinions with the forms of advertising, according to what you think.
Now work in groups. Discuss your opinions, like this:
What do you think of poster advertising?
– In my opinion it's probably quite effective, although it's unsightly./It's probably effective because it reaches a lot of people.

A	B
posters	it's effective
radio	it's unsightly
cinema	it's expensive
TV	it's ineffective
magazines	people don't listen to/watch it
newspapers	people don't go there
direct mail	people throw it/them away
brochures	it reaches a lot of/only a few people

Add more opinions and adjectives if you can.

4 Listen to the tape. You will hear an advertising manager talking about advertising certain products. First, look at Column **A** in Exercise 3 and tick (✓) the forms of advertising which the manager mentions. Then complete this chart:

	type of product	advertising form(s)	reasons for the choice
1			
2			
3			

Now listen again, and write down the three sentences which contain these words: *In spite of . . . . .*

13

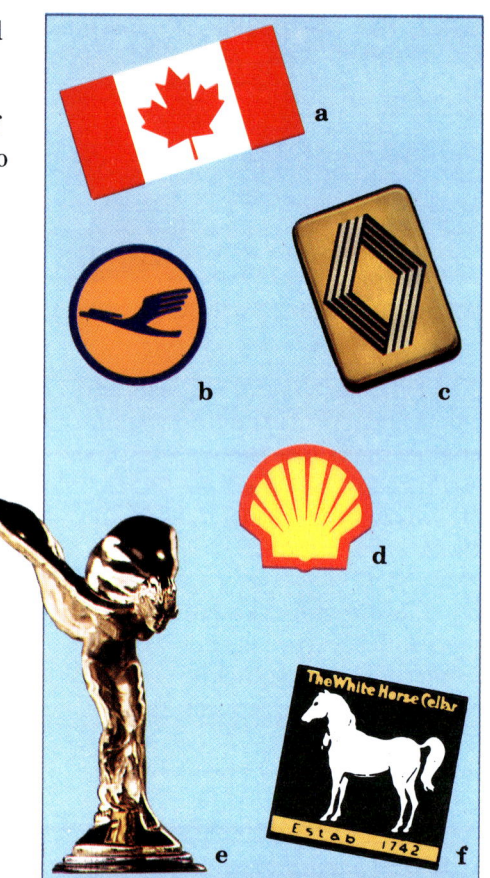

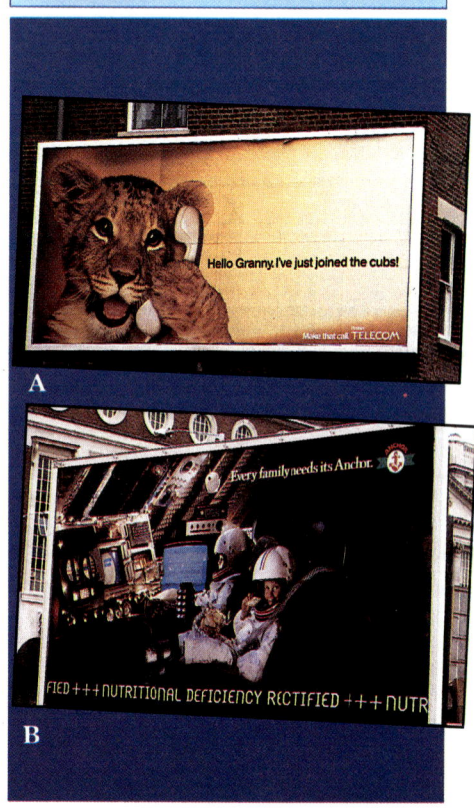

BELIEVING

5 Go back to the information in **Exercise 3** and make sentences, like this:
In spite of being unsightly, this type of advertising is good for many products like ___./In spite of the fact that many people don't go there, this type of ___.
Read your sentences to the class and ask: *Which form of advertising am I talking about?*

6 Some products are identified by numbers alone. In Column **A** on the right there are names of some famous products. In Column **B** the product is given, but only the first part of the word.
Match Columns **A** and **B** and complete the words.

A	B
No 5	comp_ _ _ _
4711	pla_ _
TR 7	col_ _ _ _
ZX 81	c_ _
VAT 69	cig_ _ _ _ _ _
555	whi_ _ _
747	perf_ _ _

7 You will now hear someone talking about advertising a perfume. As you listen, find a word or words which mean:
1 costs a lot
2 a material
3 a jewel
4 part of formal clothing for men
5 next to
6 it is successful

Summarise what you have heard by finishing this sentence:
The perfume seems good because ___.

Now discuss your answers in class:
What have you just written/said about the perfume?

8 But paintings have nothing to do with perfume. Here is a list of products and images. Match the images with the products in the chart, then, in groups of four, complete the chart for your group.
Can you tell me what is often used to advertise cars?
– Yes. I think that advertisements often use a woman in an evening dress to advertise cars.
Write the number *i, ii,* etc only under each name.

	1	2	3	4
jewellery				
wine				
ladies' fashions				
cars				
spirits (whisky, gin)				
cigarettes				
perfume				
chocolates				

i a woman in a swimming costume
ii a woman in an evening dress
iii a man in a suit
iv a wild animal
v a mountain scene
vi an outdoor man
vii a tropical island
viii mountain streams
ix ancient ruins
x a peaceful country scene

SUMMARY

Now you can:
express opinions (about advertising and the media)
express conflicting ideas

KEY GRAMMAR
Concession
In spite of being unsightly, this type of advertising is good for many products.

Make **+ infinitive without *to***
What does it make you think of?

VOCABULARY
advertising
  campaign
brochure
direct mail
image
medium (n)
poster
series

affect
recognise
think of
effective
ineffective
unsightly
visual

9 Below and on the left are advertisements for products in Britain. What do they make you think of? What products do you think the images represent? Discuss in pairs, like this:
I think A is advertising ___ .
– So do I./I don't. I think it's advertising ___ .
Now discuss as a class.

10 Work in groups. You are a marketing team. Choose a product (eg, a watch, a fur coat, chocolates,..) and decide how you want to advertise it: which methods, which images, where etc. When you have decided, write a brief report, saying what you have chosen and why. Hand your report to another group. Read the other group's report and discuss whether you agree or disagree.

A MAGNIFICENT OBSESSION WITH *colour*

Martin Zimmerli is an exciting visual artist who was born in Switzerland in 1945. Between 1959 and 1964 he studied photography and interior design at the Zürich Art and Trades School. He has lived in America since 1971. Before he decided to settle there, he had spent some time in England. He had also travelled a lot in Asia and had spent six months in Indonesia. There he was studying batik, a process which the Indonesians have practised for centuries. Since then he has used batik methods in his paintings, to express Western themes. He has been a full-time artist for many years now.

When I first met Martin he was teaching and demonstrating batik methods to interested groups. His paintings have developed since he went to America. One remarkable thing about them is their variety. They are not limited to any particular theme or subject; each one expresses his own special view of the world in a rich mixture of techniques and colours.

14

1 Read the text above and find as many sentences as you can like types A, B and C below.
A He has been in America for a long time.
B He had spent time in England before that.
C He was studying batik in Indonesia.

2 Answer these questions about the text.
1 How long had Martin lived in Switzerland before he went to Art School?
2 What had he done before he went to Indonesia?
3 Where was batik invented?
4 What was Martin doing in Indonesia?
5 Where had he spent time before he went to America?
6 What was he doing when the author met him?
7 Write a sentence about Martin now and his paintings.

3 Listen to the tape. Martin is describing the technique of batik. He mentions three materials and two tools which are necessary for batik. What are they?
Now listen to the tape again. What are the three basic steps in batik?

4 Martin lives in Boston, Massachussetts and he works in a studio near his house. He has lived and worked there since 1971.
Ask and answer in pairs like this:

Where do you live/work/shop?
What's your address?
How long have you lived/worked/
   shopped there?

Now ask other people in the class about their partners, like this:
Can you remember where ___
   lives/shops/works?
Can you remember how long he/she
   has lived/shopped/worked there?

SUMMARY

Now you can:

recall the past
describe paintings

KEY GRAMMAR
Past perfect tense
He had spent time in England before that.

Present perfect tense
How long have you lived there?

Past continuous tense
What were you doing in 1974?

Past passive
The Beatles were influenced by Elvis Presley.

VOCABULARY
batik
exhibition
influence (v)
interior design
mixture
process
technique
theme
tool
full-time

27

5 Imagine that you are an artist. Say what you were doing in each of the years below. Talk to your partner like this:
What do you do?
– I'm a painter (musician, actor, actress).
What were you doing in 1974 (between 1975 and 1977, in 1978, from 1978 to 1981, in 1982, from 1983 to the present)?

6 A few years ago the Swiss Society of Boston put on an exhibition of Swiss artists. Each of them now lives in Boston but they have all spent two months in different European countries for the last three years. Monika, for instance, went to Italy first and then to the Netherlands. She has also spent time in Spain.

	1983	1984	1985
Monika	Spain, France	Italy	Netherlands
Pierre	Scotland, Ireland	Netherlands	Sweden, Denmark
Martin	Germany, France	Italy, Austria	Switzerland

Ask and answer questions about the chart like this:
Has ___ been to ___?
– Yes, and he's also been to ___.
Has anyone been to France?
– Yes, Martin has, and Monika's been there too.

7 Ask and answer in pairs and take notes:
Where have you been? Have you ever been to ___?
– Yes, I've been to ___, and I've been to ___ too.
– No, I've never been to ___.
When was that exactly?
Now make sentences about your partner and tell the class, like this:
Before/After he had ___ he went to ___.
– When/In what year was that?
In ___./From ___ to ___./Between ___ and ___./ From ___ until ___.

8 Listen to Martin describing his six paintings. Then match the paintings with the titles below.
Rabbit Garden   Beyond the Wall   Pottery
Plans for the Sky   Joggers   The Hunters
Talk to your partner like this:
I think the first painting is called ___ because it has/there are ___.
– I think so too/ I don't agree. I think it's called ___.

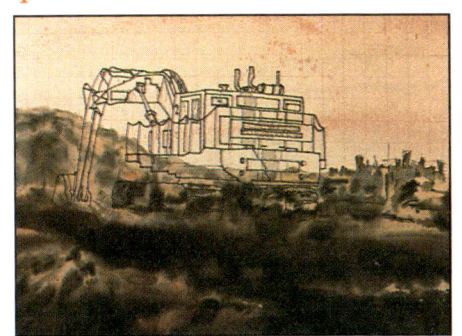

9 Here are the dates of the paintings: 1971 1974 1974 1980 1980 1985
Listen to the tape again and match the years to the paintings. Then talk to your partner like this:
When do you think Joggers was painted?
– I think it was painted in 1980, because that was when jogging became popular in the States.
What do you think he was thinking about?/What do you think it was influenced by?
– I think it was influenced by his time in ___.
Use the text and the tapescript to help you.

10 Quiz. The Mona Lisa was painted by Leonardo da Vinci, the Beatles were influenced by Elvis Presley, Macbeth was written by Shakespeare. Everyone knows these. In groups make a list of up to ten books, paintings, musical compositions, artists. Then ask other groups like this:
Who was ___ written/ painted/ influenced by?

14

15

Colour Talks

Black is —— and ——. It's the colour that ——. Everyone can wear black.

It used to be called wine or maroon; now —— burgundy, named after ——. It's a colour that you associate with —— and it looks lovely against —— with ——.

Pink is a ——. It's the colour that —— if you want ——.

Midnight blue is another name that ——; it's for ——. It's also very —— and —— with white and red.

Red is the colour that —— when you want attention. Don't wear it if ——.

White means —— and ——. It looks —— and —— in winter, and —— and —— in summer. It's very flattering.

Grey is ——. If grey is the colour that ——, —— wear other colours with it.

Another dramatic colour is ——. It's gorgeous and precious. It —— by blondes, redheads or brunettes and it can go ——.

Colour is a very important part of life. Every time we buy anything, our choice may be influenced by colour. Colour can attract you like a magnet. It can affect the way you look and feel. Colour is used by designers and advertisers, psychologists and decorators, artists and architects. In fact, the colour you choose to wear says something about you, how you feel, and how you want others to feel about you. In other words, colour talks.

1 Listen to the tape and complete the sentences in the picture above.

2 *Midnight blue is another name that you can use for navy.* You can also say this sentence without *that*. Look at the chart and the colours on the right. Work in pairs. Student A points to a colour and asks a question and Student B replies, like this:
What colour is this?
– *That's burgundy. It's another name you can use for maroon.*

A	B
	1 burgundy/maroon
	2 aquamarine/turquoise
	3 scarlet/bright red
	4 chocolate/dark brown
	5 mauve/light purple
	6 mustard/dark yellow
	7 khaki/brownish yellow
	8 midnight blue/navy
	9 rust/reddish brown
	10 beige/light brown
	11 peach/pinkish orange

29

3 Burgundy is a colour that you associate with royalty. What do colours make you think of? What do you associate them with? Using the colours in Exercise 2, ask and answer in pairs, like this:
What does burgundy make you think of?
– Burgundy is a colour I associate with royalty.

4 Look at Columns **A** and **B** and match the colours with their meanings.

A	B
blue	tranquillity
red	strength
pink	generosity
white	femininity
green	purity
brown	love
orange	mystery
violet	romance
turquoise	seriousness

Now listen to what the experts say these colours mean.
Were you right, or do you disagree? Now try and remember the *adjectives* used on the tape to describe the colours above, e.g. blue = feminine. Listen to the tape again. Were you correct?

SUMMARY

Now you can:

talk about colours
give definitions
give explanations

KEY GRAMMAR
Deleted relative pronoun *that*
Midnight blue is another name you can use for navy.

Emphatic *do/does*
That *does* look nice!

Was going to
I *was* going to paint it white, but I've changed my mind.

VOCABULARY
attention   fashionable
affect (v)   flattering
associate with   sophisticated
dramatic

5 You are planning the colour scheme for a house. Choose a colour for each room and fill in the table below. Say why you have chosen each colour.
What colour have you chosen for the study? – White.
Why? – It'll make the room look bigger.
Here are some adjectives you can use:
cheerful light bright warm
cool severe spacious dramatic
romantic tranquil

Room	Colour(s)	Reasons
living room		
kitchen		
dining room		
children's bedroom		
main bedroom		
study	white	bigger
bathroom		

6 Now work in pairs. You are a newly married couple, who have just bought a new house. You're going to decorate it from top to bottom. You have both made plans for this without talking to the other. Now discuss the colour scheme, like this:
I'm going to paint the study white.
– Why?
It'll make the room look bigger.
– All right then. That's a good idea.
– No, I don't like/can't stand/hate white. How about blue?
Try to reach agreement.

7 You meet another couple at a dinner party. Tell them about your plans, like this:
We're decorating our new house from top to bottom.
– Oh, really? What colour have you chosen for ___?
Well, I was going to paint it white, to look bigger, but I've changed my mind. We're going to paint it bright pink now, to look cheerful.
– What colour have you chosen ___?
Six months later you see your new friends again. You take them round your newly decorated house. Make conversation like this:
And this is the study. We were going to paint...
– Oh! That does look nice!

8 Here is a list of public buildings. Write down what colour you associate with each one, and why.
hospital church disco
Chinese restaurant school
post office butcher's baker's
nightclub library

9 Work in groups. Look at the photographs below and describe them. Talk about skin, eyes and hair, like this:
Helmut's got blue eyes, blond hair, and a fair complexion.
Now decide what colour(s) each person should wear. Finally, report back to the class: *We think Helmut should wear blue because he's got blue eyes, blond hair, and a fair complexion.*

Sonia

Helmut

Nicki

15

30

OPERATION RALEIGH

High, cold mountains, dry deserts, humid jungles, and the open ocean – these are areas of the earth which will be visited by the *Sir Walter Raleigh* in a four-year journey round the world. The ship, which is a 1,900 ton sailing ship, is the headquarters for about 4,000 young men and women, who come from the UK and USA, and other countries. Each of them joins the expedition for about three months. All of them have been carefully selected, because conditions are uncomfortable and the work is often difficult. *Operation Raleigh* has been organised to give young people the opportunity not only of adventure but also of doing valuable community work and scientific research.

1 Read the text and then ask and answer questions in pairs, like this:
Where in the world can you find: high mountains/deserts/jungles?
Can you give me the name of any mountains in ___ (country)?
Can you give me the name of a desert in ___ (country)?

2 Look at this sentence: *These adventurers have been carefully selected.*
Here are some actions and some reasons. Match Columns **A** and **B** and ask and answer questions, like this:
Why have the adventurers been carefully selected?
– They have been carefully selected because the work is difficult.

A	B
adventurers/carefully select	people want to learn more about the jungle
new underground system/build	the work is difficult
man/send/to hospital	the traffic is very heavy
young woman/choose/for the job	he is extremely ill
expedition/organise	she is the best candidate
research/do	we need to find a cure for the disease

3 Complete the following sentences in your own words.
The *Sir Walter Raleigh*, which is a 1,900 ton sailing ship, is the headquarters for 4,000 young people.
1 The Gobi desert, which is one of the largest ___, is in Mongolia.
2 The Nile, which is one of the largest ___, is in Egypt.
3 Antarctica, which at one time was much ___, is one of the continents.
4 The Himalayas, which contain most ___, are in Tibet and Nepal.

Now ask and answer questions, like this:
I know that the Sir Walter Raleigh is the headquarters for 4,000 young people, but can you tell me something more?
– Yes. It's a 1,900 ton sailing ship.

4 Look at the map and timetable, and then ask and answer questions like this:
Where will the ship be/was the ship in ___?
– In ___/From ___ to ___ the ship will be/was in ___.
How long will/did it take from ___ to ___?
– It will take/took ___.

Operation Raleigh Approximate Timetable

	Arrive	Depart
Great Britain		Nov 1984
Bahamas	Dec 1984	Mar 1985
Honduras	Apr 1985	June 1985
Chile (Santiago) or Falkland Islands	July 1985	Dec 1985
Tonga	Oct 1985	Dec 1985
Papua – New Guinea	Mar 1986	May 1986
New Zealand	May 1986	Aug 1986
Japan	Oct 1986	Feb 1987
Sri Lanka	Apr 1987	June 1987
Kenya	July 1987	Nov 1987
Cameroun or Brazil (Rio)	Jan 1988	May 1988
Venezuela (Caracas)	May 1988	Aug 1988
Great Britain	June 1988	Sep 1988
	Oct 1988	Dec 1988
	Dec 1988	

5 The Sir Walter Raleigh is stopping at several towns and countries during the four-year journey. Ask and answer questions in pairs, like this:
The ship stops in South America. Does it stop in Rio?
– No, it only stops in ___.
– Yes. It stops not only in Rio but also in Santiago.
Ask and answer about yourselves:
Have you ever crossed the Mediterranean?
– Yes, I've crossed not only the Mediterranean but also the Atlantic.

6 In spring 1985 a news update on some of the projects was given out. On the tape you will hear the difficult names from the middle column below. Listen and write the order in which they are said in the left-hand column. Then listen to the news update and complete the notes.

	Grand Bahama	**Main objective =** ___
	Breeding of fish	Experiments have ___
	Lucayan National Park	There have been ___
1	Mapping of seagrass	Experiments have ___
	Turks and Caicos Islands	**Main objective =** ___
	North Caicos	The basketball court ___
	Middle Caicos	Sea divers are ___
	Grand Turk	The most important work on ___

7 In groups, make a list of projects which have been completed over the last ten years in your town/country. Here is a list of projects. Add some more of your own.
theatre or culture centres   shopping centres
underground systems   dams   motorways   city parks
Ask and answer, like this:
Can you think of any major projects that have been built/completed/started over the last few years?

Now change groups and ask and answer, like this:
In ___ the following projects have been ___ over the last few years.
– When was the ___ started/completed?
In ___./I don't know.

Write a paragraph about the other group, like this:
A new shopping centre in ___ has been started and so has a ___. During the last ___ years, they have not only built a ___ but also a ___.

8 A real problem with *Operation Raleigh* is funding – finding the money. In 1984 it cost £2,800 for each adventurer, and this is so high that the adventurers have been asked to try to find some of this money themselves. Listen to the tape and you will hear certain ways in which the operation is being helped. Answer the questions and then complete the sentences below in your own words, or the words from the tape.
1 What does a sponsor do?   2 What is a donation?
3 Have you ever made a donation?   4 What was it?

Local sponsors   The adventurers are ___.
Industry   Many companies, such as ___ have ___.
Equipment   Some people ___.
Donations   The operation also ___ throughout ___.

9 In groups interview a person who wants to join the operation. Ask about background, interests and ability to contribute (skills and knowledge).

SUMMARY

Now you can:
talk about the world in generalisations

KEY GRAMMAR
Present perfect passive
The adventurers have been carefully selected.

Non-defining relatives: *which*
The ship, which is a 1,900 ton sailing ship, is the
    headquarters . . .

VOCABULARY
adventure	experiment	donate
community work	headquarters	fund
continent	jungle	organise
desert	project	select
expedition	sponsor (n)	sponsor (v)

16

ADOPT AN ANIMAL
AT LONDON ZOO

From now on your visits to London Zoo can be even more exciting and worthwhile. Because this is your chance not only to see one of the largest collections of wild animals in the world, but also to visit your very own animal.

Every animal (and there are more than 8,000 at London Zoo), from lemurs to leopards, bats to badgers, is waiting to be adopted. By you or your family. By a school class or club. Or even by a company.

In fact our Adopt an Animal Scheme is open to anyone or any group with a love of animals and an interest in saving the world's wildlife from further loss.

1 Find words or phrases in the text which mean:
support financially   from today
not a waste of time   rescuing
all animals which are not domestic

2 Match Column **A** and Column **B** and write sentences like these:
London Zoo has one of the largest collections of wild animals.
The QEII is one of the largest ___.

A	B
The Louvre	populations
Disneyland	amusement parks
India	collections of paintings
The Victoria and Albert Museum	collections of costumes
The Empire State Building	collections of wild animals
Kenya	ocean liners
London Zoo	wildlife parks
The QEII	buildings

Now ask people to guess what you are talking about, like this:
It has one of the largest collections of animals in the world. What is it?
– Is it London Zoo?

Why you should think about adopting.

3 Someone from the Adopt an Animal office is giving reasons for the scheme. Listen and write down the reasons in the spaces below. Now ask your partner questions about the reasons, like this:
What did she say about London Zoo?
– She said it was one of the most famous zoos in the world.
1 London Zoo ___.
2 Together with ___ it ___.
3 ___ no money of its own and ___.
4 Many of its animals ___.
5 And most of the animals ___.
6 If ___ it ___.

4 You have just completed reasons why you should think about adopting.
Now look at these statements in pairs and find reasons why you should or shouldn't do these things.
visit the dentist
not buy a sports car
not watch too much TV
not eat meat
live in the country
buy a computer

Now choose one topic and write a paragraph about it.

How the adopt an animal scheme works.

The amount needed to keep and feed an animal for one year is broken down into adoption units of £30. For example, it costs just about £30 a year to keep a Philippine cloud rat. So, if you bought one £30 adoption unit you could adopt a cloud rat for one whole year. On the other hand, a lion costs around £1,500. So if you paid £30, you could buy one of the 50 adoption units available for each lion in the zoo. If you'd like to buy all 170 units and adopt an elephant, we'd be delighted – and so would the elephant. If you are interested in adopting one of the very small animals, adoption units will cost only £10 a year.

SUMMARY

Now you can:
explain and describe emotions
categorise animals

KEY GRAMMAR
Superlatives
London zoo has one of the largest collections of wild animals.

Improbable condition
How would you feel if smoking was banned?

VOCABULARY
category   reptile
insect   wildlife
mammal   complimentary
marsupial   worthwhile

17

33

5 Look at this sentence from the text: *If you'd like to ... adopt an elephant, we'd be delighted – and so would the elephant.* *Delighted* means *very, very happy*. Put these adjectives in order of happiness: miserable delighted unconcerned pleased happy unhappy dissatisfied

6 Work in groups. Look at the situations below. How would you feel if your home football team lost a match? Choose one of the adjectives from Exercise 5, or one of those below for each situation.
Other adjectives: annoyed angry furious upset shocked surprised
Now discuss your answers with other groups, like this:
How would you/Elena feel if smoking was banned?
– I'd/She'd feel annoyed.

smoking was banned
all zoos were closed
eating meat was made illegal
a woman became president/prime minister
hunting was stopped
no one could play golf at weekends
divorce was forbidden

7 Look at the lists of animals on the right, choose ten that you don't recognise and look them up in the dictionary. Decide which of the categories below they belong to. (You might need to look these up, too.)
marsupials insects reptiles birds farm animals cats polar animals water animals
Now ask others in the class about your animals like this:
Do you know what a kangaroo is?
– Yes, it's a marsupial and it's found in Australia.
– No, I don't. What is it?
Does anybody/do you know any other marsupials?

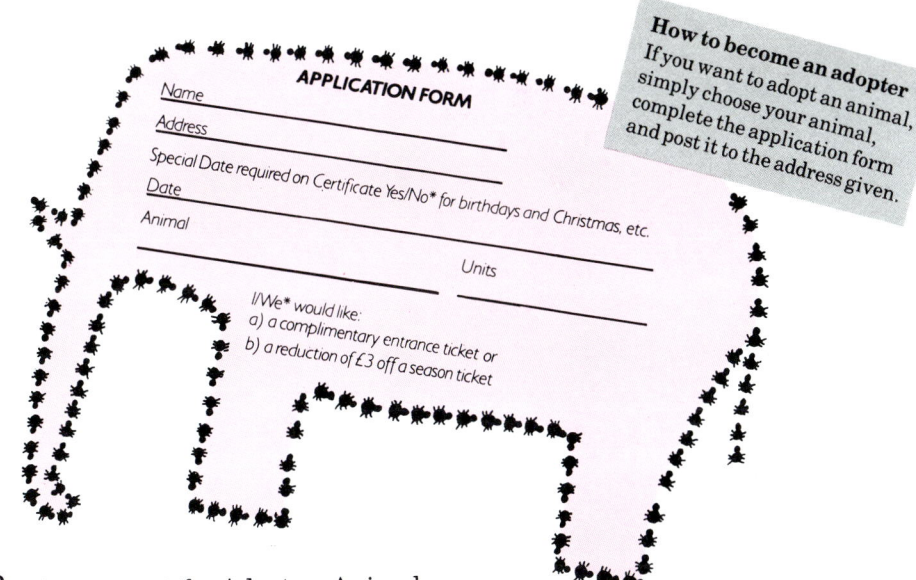

APPLICATION FORM
Name
Address
Special Date required on Certificate Yes/No* for birthdays and Christmas, etc.
Date
Animal
Units
I/We* would like:
a) a complimentary entrance ticket or
b) a reduction of £3 off a season ticket

How to become an adopter
If you want to adopt an animal, simply choose your animal, complete the application form and post it to the address given.

8 Someone at the Adopt an Animal office is helping Mrs Harrison to complete the application form. Listen to the tape and complete the questions she asks below.
1 May I have ___?
2 What is your ___?
3 Is it a ___?
4 What is her ___?
5 Do you want ___?
6 Which ___?
7 Would you like to ___ or ___?

9 Some animals are no longer available for adoption because the units have been taken up. Work in pairs. Student A reads the information in Box **A** on the right; Student B reads Box **B**.
Act out the situation. Start like this:
B *Hello, is that Mr/Mrs ___? This is the Adopt an Animal office.*

A
You want to adopt a cockatoo, and have sent an application form and £30. You don't want a common animal, like a hedgehog, and you don't want a cheaper animal because they're all fairly common. You could pay £60 but you're not very happy about it. Decide on an animal with the representative from Adopt an Animal.

B
You work for Adopt an Animal. You have an application form for a cockatoo in front of you, but there are no more units left. Ring the person up and make the following suggestions: Another animal for £30 (use the list below); a cheaper animal; an animal for £60. Use the list to find out which animals remain.

Which animal did you decide on?

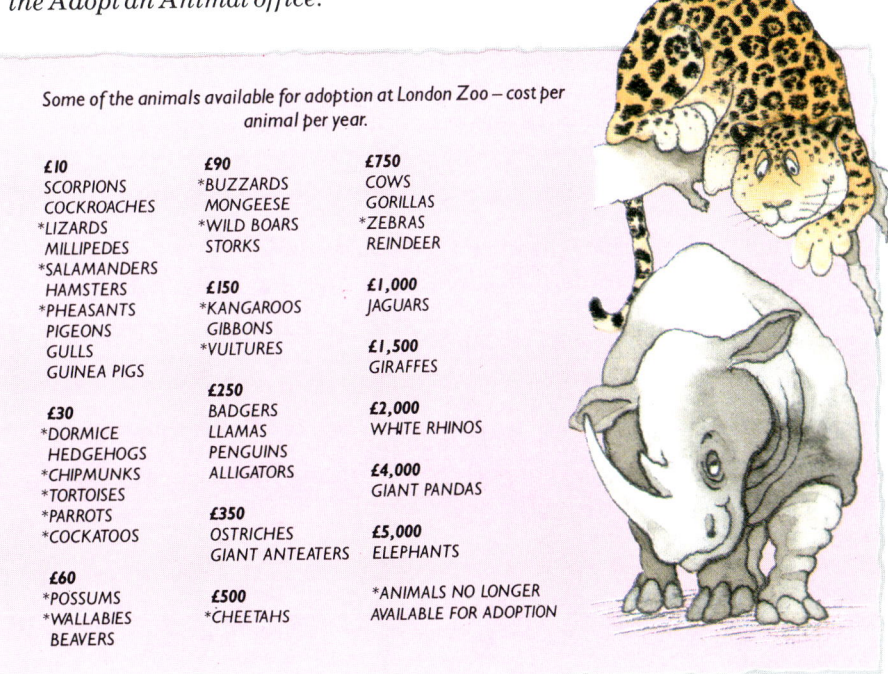

Some of the animals available for adoption at London Zoo – cost per animal per year.

£10	£90	£750
SCORPIONS	*BUZZARDS	COWS
COCKROACHES	MONGEESE	GORILLAS
*LIZARDS	*WILD BOARS	*ZEBRAS
MILLIPEDES	STORKS	REINDEER
*SALAMANDERS		
HAMSTERS	£150	£1,000
*PHEASANTS	*KANGAROOS	JAGUARS
PIGEONS	GIBBONS	
GULLS	*VULTURES	£1,500
GUINEA PIGS		GIRAFFES
	£250	
£30	BADGERS	£2,000
*DORMICE	LLAMAS	WHITE RHINOS
HEDGEHOGS	PENGUINS	
*CHIPMUNKS	ALLIGATORS	£4,000
*TORTOISES		GIANT PANDAS
*PARROTS	£350	
*COCKATOOS	OSTRICHES	£5,000
	GIANT ANTEATERS	ELEPHANTS
£60		
*POSSUMS	£500	*ANIMALS NO LONGER
*WALLABIES	*CHEETAHS	AVAILABLE FOR ADOPTION
BEAVERS		

17

34

A Kind of Medicine

When you feel very ill, you may go to the doctor. The doctor is highly trained in medicine, which is a good thing, and he will probably treat you with conventional medicine of some sort. This is orthodox medicine. But there are other sorts of medicine and many of these have been around for hundreds of years. These are known as alternative medicine, such as nutritional medicine, eating the right food, and medical herbalism, using herbs as medicine, to give just two examples. For a long time orthodox doctors, and much of the public, have been cautious of this form of medicine. But this seems to be changing, as a recent survey shows. Many orthodox doctors have changed their minds about alternative medicine; quite a few recommend it to their patients, when orthodox medicine doesn't work; some doctors even practise it. When the doctors who do not practise it were asked 'Would you like to?' a majority (57 per cent) answered that they would.

1 Read the passage above and find the opposites of the following words:
unusual   orthodox medicine   warn against   minority

2 Read the passage again and answer the questions below.
1 What is *a good thing* (line 2)? That ___.
2 What is orthodox medicine? When ___.
3 Give two examples of alternative medicine.
4 What does *this form of medicine* refer to (line 6)?
5 What *seems to be changing* (line 6)?
6 How has it changed?
7 Who would like to practise alternative medicine?

The charts on the right show the results of the survey on how doctors have changed their minds about alternative medicine.

3 Listen to the tape and complete the pie charts by placing a symbol next to the correct percentage. For example, the researcher on the tape says that 11 per cent of those who became doctors before 1969 have a strong disbelief. So you place a ▲ in the top pie chart next to 11 per cent.

4 Here are some more examples of alternative medicine:
acupuncture   meditation   healing   hypnotherapy
They come from these words: puncture   meditate   heal   hypnotise
Ask other members in the class about the words you don't know, like this:
I don't know what 'heal' means, do you?
—I think it means (native word)/*making people well by faith in God.*

5 On the right is a list of common complaints which can be treated with alternative medicine. With your partner look up any words you do not know. Then in groups of three ask and answer like this:
Do you smoke/have any phobias?
—No, I don't, but I do suffer from depression/Yes I do. I smoke twenty a day/I'm afraid of snakes. Can you tell me what to do for it?
I should ___.
Why don't you ___?

WHAT THE DOCTORS THINK
How they have changed their minds

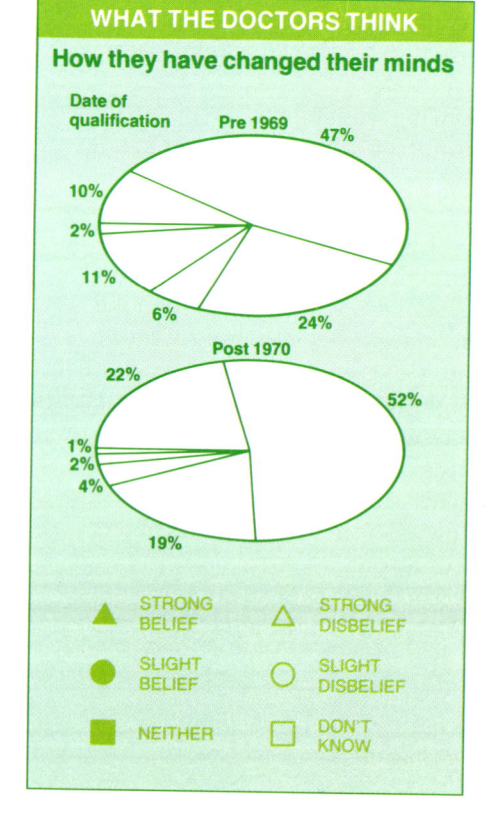

Date of qualification

Pre 1969: 47%, 10%, 2%, 11%, 6%, 24%

Post 1970: 22%, 52%, 1%, 2%, 4%, 19%

- ▲ STRONG BELIEF
- △ STRONG DISBELIEF
- ● SLIGHT BELIEF
- ○ SLIGHT DISBELIEF
- ■ NEITHER
- ☐ DON'T KNOW

smoking	stress
anxiety	tension
phobias	depression
obesity	insomnia
asthma	headache

6 Read **An Expert's View** on the right. Professor Sinclair mentions some advantages and some disadvantages of both orthodox and alternative medicine. He says: 'Doctors who practise alternative medicine … listen to their patients. That is a very good thing.' He could also have said:
Doctors who practise alternative medicine listen to their patients, which is a good thing.
Find the other advantages and disadvantages and write some sentences following the same pattern.
In groups, discuss the following questions:
What is the advantage of alternative medicine?
Are there any disadvantages?

7 Here are some other situations which may be good or bad, but not everyone may agree. What do you think? Make sentences from the table, beginning: *In my country ____.*

The Government pays/doesn't pay for health care, The shops close/don't close on Sundays, Children are/aren't allowed in bars or pubs, One-parent families receive/don't receive money/help from the Government, There is a/no speed limit on the motorways, There are only ____ national holidays a year,	which is	good. bad. terrible. lovely. inconvenient. not enough. unfair.

Write five more things which you think are good, bad, unfair, etc. and then compare opinions with other people in the class, like this:
The Government in England pays for health care, which is very good.
– I agree/I disagree. I think it's unfair.

An Expert's View

Alternative medicine is a confusing term. In both orthodox and alternative medicine there are treatments which work and treatments which may not always work. Sometimes a patient may not find the orthodox treatment satisfactory. Then doctors can recommend an alternative treatment. This is very good. Doctors, as we all know, have very little time. They often prescribe a medicine without saying very much to their patients. One of the greatest advantages of doctors who practise alternative medicine is that they spend a great deal of time listening to their patients. That is also a very good thing. Orthodox doctors should also be doing this. On the other hand we can be certain that an orthodox doctor has received proper training in orthodox medicine, under proper supervision. This is not always true of the other doctors. The Government does not recognise alternative medicine and there is no proper regulation. Many doctors who are beginning to practise alternative medicine are not qualified to do so, and this is not a good thing. But there is nothing to stop them.

Professor A J Sinclair
St Marie's Hospital

18

SUMMARY

Now you can:

explain meanings of words
talk about advantages and disadvantages

KEY GRAMMAR
Relative clause *which* referring to whole clause
In my country, the shops close on Sundays, which is inconvenient.

Is good for/Is used for
The juice of half an orange is good for/is used for hiccoughs.

VOCABULARY
acupuncture
depression
hiccoughs
insomnia
meditation
practise

treat

alternative
conventional
orthodox
trained

8 Medical herbalism is a popular form of alternative medicine. Look at the list of problems and the list of treatments below. With your partner match Columns **A** and **B** like this:
I don't know what to do for ____. Do you know what is good for ____?
Do you know how to treat ____?
– I think ____ is good for/used for ____.

A	B
bad breath	CINNAMON IN HOT MILK AND HONEY
colds	ORANGE JUICE OR ONION JUICE
cuts	LEMON JUICE
nausea	SAGE TEA WITH VINEGAR
depression	PEPPERMINT TEA OR FRESH PARSLEY
earache	HOT HONEY AND LEMON JUICE
hiccoughs	LIME TEA
insomnia	POWDERED GINGER
sore throat	OATS
travel sickness	GARLIC CREAM

Now listen to the tape. Were you right?

9 In groups decide on home remedies for the common problems in Exercise 8. Talk to each other like this and take notes.
Do you know what to do for headaches?
– Aspirin is used for/is good for headaches, but it makes you sleepy, which is a bad thing.
I don't like using aspirin, but I do like ____.
Now write a short paragraph about the remedies you discussed in your group.

MOVERS
how mobile are you?

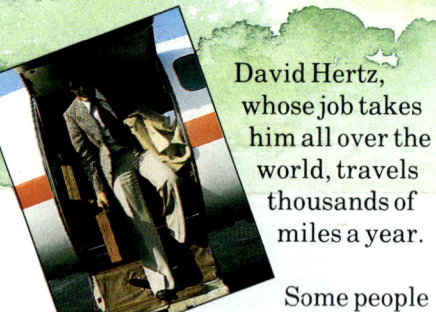

David Hertz, whose job takes him all over the world, travels thousands of miles a year.

Some people fly only once or twice in their lives, but David Hertz, who runs his own company, flies thousands of miles every month of the year. His company, which makes hospital equipment, sells in over fifty countries and David is away from home nearly two weeks a month. We spoke to his wife, who hates flying and has only once been on a plane.

1 Look at the text and identify the sentences with these words:
who   which   whose

Complete these sentences in your own words:
1 John Hunt, who ____, is a good friend of mine.
2 His company, which ____, is in Düsseldorf.
3 My sister, whose boyfriend ____, lives in Oslo.
4 My car, which ____, is ten years old.
5 Mary Hertz, whose husband ____, has only flown once.

2 Now listen to Mary Hertz talking, and complete these sentences:
1 She ____ count ____.
2 But she doesn't ____.
3 Her husband ____ but now ____.
4 She ____ all the time.
5 She used to think ____.

3 David Hertz travels over 300,000 km a year on business. Complete this chart for yourself then complete it for your partner. Ask questions, like this:
How many km do/did you ____?
How many planes have you ____?

	You	Your partner
km/from work/home (travel)		
km/at weekends (travel)		
km/on your last holiday (travel)		
planes in your life (take)		
homes in the last 15 years (live in)		

4 David Hertz does not suffer from jet lag. Here are some things people suffer from, especially when they travel:
fear of flying   agoraphobia
vertigo   travel sickness
sea sickness   claustrophobia
(Look up words you don't know in your dictionaries.)
Now ask and answer questions, like this:
Do you know anyone who suffers from sea sickness?
– Yes, an aunt of mine, who lives in Brazil, suffers from sea sickness.
Do you suffer from ____?
– No, I don't, but a friend of mine, whose name is ____, suffers from ____.

Now write two sentences, like this:
My friend, who suffers from claustrophobia, never goes on the underground.

5 The boxes below tell what happened to two people in a twenty-year period, but the information about one of them is incomplete. Ask your partner questions about the second person and fill in the blanks.

A
Pierre is a marketing manager who lives in Paris. He used to work for an advertising company. Now he works for a large department store and he has worked there for fourteen years. He has lived in Paris for the last 20 years.

Dr. Suzuki, who is from ____, is a ____. She has worked for ____ for the last ____. She lives in ____ now but she used to live in Kyoto from 1961 to ____ and then in ____, from ____ to ____.

B
Dr. Suzuki, who is from Japan, is a scientist. She has worked for a large computer company for the last twenty years. She lives in Tokyo now, but she used to live in Kyoto from 1961 to 1964 and then in Osaka, from 1965 to 1972.

Pierre is a ____ who lives in ____. He used to work for ____. Now he works for ____ and he has worked there for ____. He has lived in Paris ____.

6 Here are some companies. Do you know which country they started in? Do you know what they make? Ask and answer, like this:
What do you know about ITT?
– ITT, which is American, makes satellites.

ITT   Heineken   Toyota   Boeing
XEROX   Hoover   IBM   BP   Fiat
Heinz   Texas Instruments
Rothmans   Dunlop   Philips

7 Make sentences like the example. Write them down.
Freda, whose husband works for the German Embassy, lives in Bangkok.

1	Freda	German Embassy	Bangkok
2	Maria	General Electric	New York
3	Ram	British Airways	New Delhi
4	Anna	Polish Government	Krakow
5	Harry	BBC	London
6	Arthur	the Sorbonne	Paris

Now ask and answer questions, like this:
Who lives in New York?
– Maria does.
Whose wife works for the BBC?
– Harry's does.
Write two sentences about people you know and tell the class, like this:
My aunt, whose husband is a sea captain, lives in Alaska.

8 Some people move house several times, too. Listen to the tape. You will hear an American woman being interviewed about the number of times she and her husband have moved.
1 Name the five States which the people have lived in.
2 Where did they live first?
3 Where did they live after that?
4 Where do they live now?
5 What does her husband do?
6 Which State did she like the best?

Listen to the woman again and write the sentences with the words *except for* and *including*.

9 Make sentences, using *except for* and *including* (your answers don't have to be true), like this:
Have you been to any countries in Asia (Europe, Africa . . .)?
– I've been to several countries in Asia (Europe, Africa . . .), including ___.
– I haven't been to any countries in ___, except for ___.
Have you been to any towns in ___?
– I've been to several towns in ___, including ___.
– I haven't been to any towns in ___, except for ___.
– I've not only been to ___ in ___, but also to ___.

10 Survey: How mobile are you? Work in groups of four to complete the chart below.
Report to the class like this.
One of the people in our group has visited ___ countries, lived in ___ towns and held ___ jobs. Who do you think it is?

11 Do you think your country has a very mobile society? Write a paragraph about it.
Use these words: most   a lot of
very few   hardly any   frequently

SUMMARY

Now you can:
talk about travel
give information about people

KEY GRAMMAR
Non-defining relatives:
who   whose
David Hertz, who runs his own company, travels thousands of miles . . .
Freda, whose husband works for the German Embassy, lives in Bangkok.

Except for/including
I've never been out of the States, except for Hawaii.
We've lived in four States, including New York.

VOCABULARY
jet lag   run (a company)
sea sickness   suffer from
move house   mobile

19

		1	2	3	4
Number of	countries visited				
	countries lived in				
	jobs held				
	schools attended				
	towns lived in				
	houses/flats lived in				
	plane journeys a year				

MISSING

As many as 25,000 people in Britain go missing each year. Most of them come back but some never do. Michael Dean is one of these. He disappeared during a visit to the fair three years ago with his mother and sister, and has never been seen since. His parents still hope that he may return home one day, alive and well.

20

1 Read the text above and answer these questions.
1. When and where was Michael Dean last seen?
2. In your own words, say what happened to Michael.
3. Complete these sentences:
   Above is a photograph of _____ where _____
   Michael Dean is a boy who _____

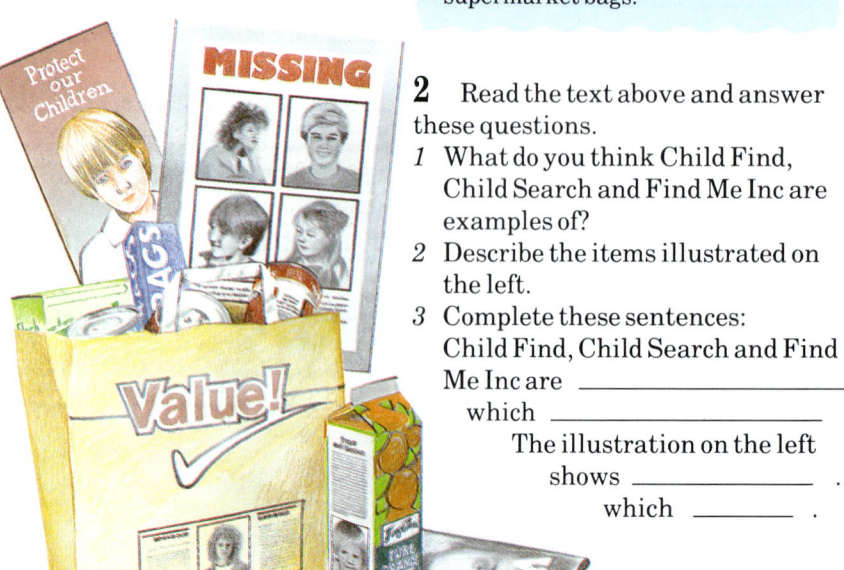

In America an estimated 1.8 million children go missing each year. There are several organisations which try to find missing children. They publish magazines with photographs and details of the children, booklets to help parents, and one organisation puts photographs on cardboard milk cartons and on paper supermarket bags.

2 Read the text above and answer these questions.
1. What do you think Child Find, Child Search and Find Me Inc are examples of?
2. Describe the items illustrated on the left.
3. Complete these sentences:
   Child Find, Child Search and Find Me Inc are _____ which _____ .
   The illustration on the left shows _____ which _____ .

3 Mrs X is a woman who has lost her memory. No one knows her name.
Listen to the tape and answer the questions below.
1. Who were the man and woman in white?
2. Where are the interviewer and Mrs X?
3. What do you think happened to Mrs X?
4. What examples of identification does the interviewer give?
5. Who do you think Ron was?

4 These days parents worry a lot about the health and the safety of their children. Some are very strict with their children to try to protect them from all possible dangers. Sally Turner is eleven years old, and an only child. Her parents have made some rules to try to make sure she comes to no harm. Look at the table on the facing page. In Column **A** are the rules they have made; in Column **B** are the reasons for them.

39

A	B
Can't go out after dark.	Won't spend it sensibly.
Mustn't play near the river.	It'll take away her appetite.
Can't watch TV after 7.30 pm.	Are bad for her teeth.
Mustn't eat sweets.	Programmes may be violent.
Mustn't eat between meals.	Might be attacked.
Can't have any pocket money.	May fall in and drown.
Mustn't come home from school alone.	Might be kidnapped.
Can't ride a bicycle on the road.	May have an accident.
Can't go horse riding.	May fall off and hurt herself.

Work in pairs. One person plays the part of Sally and the other is Sally's father. Match Columns **A** and **B**, and ask and answer like this:
Why won't you let me go out after dark?
– Because you might be attacked.
Now write sentences like this:
They won't let her go out after dark because she might be attacked.

5 Survey. In all countries, the government makes rules or laws, to protect the individual, but these laws vary from country to country. Work in groups and find out about the laws of other countries like this:
At what age do they let you ___ in Germany?
Find out when you can do the following:
ride a motorbike   leave school
get married   have the vote
drive a car   retire   buy cigarettes
drink in a bar

> In Britain as many as 25,000 people go missing every year. How do police try to find a missing person?

6 Listen to the tape and write down the five sentences as you hear them. Then add *who(m)*, *which*, or *where* to each sentence.

7 Now listen to an American policeman describing how they try to find a missing person there, and answer these questions.
1 Does the policeman say APB or ABP?
2 What word is used instead of mother/father?
3 Give three examples of 'media' in the tape.

4 How many children go missing in the USA each year?
Look at the sentences you wrote in Exercise 6 and put them in the same order as they occur on the tape.

8 If you lose your memory today, do you have any identification? How will the police (or others) know who you are? Write a paragraph about the things in your pockets (wallet, handbag, briefcase), like this:
I've got a driving licence which lets them know my name, address and telephone number. I've also got ___.

9 Match Column **A** with Column **B** below and ask and answer questions about your country or a country your partner knows about:
In ___, is it possible to drive a car without your licence?
– Of course it is./Of course not.

10 Make a list of any six items like this: *wallet, credit card, cheque book, US currency, address book, ID card* and give it to your partner. Now ask and answer questions, like this:
How many of these have you got on you?
– I haven't got any except for ___./I've got everything except for ___./I've got hardly any of these, only the ___.
Change partners and repeat.

A	B
drive a car	your ID
have a bank account	passing a medical test
get a passport	your birth certificate
get a car licence	passing your test
join the army	your licence
change foreign money	your passport
go into a bar	telling the tax man

SUMMARY

Now you can:

describe purpose of objects
talk about possibility
reply or deny emphatically

KEY GRAMMAR
Except for
I haven't got any except for a cheque book.

Let
Why won't you let me go out after dark?

VOCABULARY
fair
identification
milk carton
poster

estimated
strict

contact (v)
drown
kidnap
wander about

20

40

Sports Beat

1 Complete these words:

impo____nce   equip_____   w__dy

expe_____nce   p____ch_te   w_tsu__

su__bo____   p___asa___ing

2 Fill in the missing verbs in these sentences.

1 When you go into strange places to find things out you e....................

2 People do this from parachutes. H....................

3 You r.................... the waves on a surfboard.

4 When you find something new you d.................... it.

5 If you want to become very good at something it's necessary to p.................... .

3 Change the following sentences into direct speech. Write what the people really said, like this:

He said that it's warmer than his old wetsuit.
'It's warmer than my old wetsuit.'

1 She told me that flying was her favourite sport.

....

2 They said that they liked surfboarding.

....

3 I told him to be very careful in the caves.

....

4 Yannis said that a lot of people go parasailing every day.

....

5 Photos told us that he combines business with pleasure.

....

4 Finish these conditions:

1 If you don't work hard, you can't ....

2 If you don't practise every day, you ....

3 .... you can't go parasailing.

....

4 .... you can't go horse riding.

5 .... you can go a lot faster.

6 ...., you'll be in much better shape.

5 Make five sentences from the chart, like this:
Arne is a Norwegian who lives in Tromso.

Gunter is an Austrian who is married to a German.

	Nationality	Town	Married to
Arne	Norwegian	Tromso	Englishwoman
Lennart	Swede	Malmo	Frenchwoman
Gunter	Austrian	Linz	German
Christian	Dane	Copenhagen	Swiss woman
Margareta	Finn	Turku	Dutchman
Bruce	Scot	Inverness	Irish woman

1 ....

2 ....

3 ....

4 ....

5 ....

6 Decide which adjective describes which sport.

exciting   dangerous   boring   expensive   easy   difficult   safe

windsurfing ....

horse riding ....

parasailing ....

swimming ....

playing golf ....

mountain climbing ....

skiing ....

41

Does the child make the man?

1 Complete these words:

int__vi__   occ__at____   ed__ati__

trai_in_   cho____   _pp____un__ie_

d__or____   cen____y

2 Fill in the missing verbs in these sentences.

1 When you get older as a child you g............ u............ .

2 When you are old and leave work you r............ .

3 Jennifer Nicholls s............ two years in France.

4 For some types of job, for example, a doctor or a teacher, you need to t............ .

5 Sometimes you want to buy something, but you can't because you don't have enough money. In this case, we say that you can't a............ it.

3 Write sentences about the people below, like the example.

Maria/leave school/next year/dental nurse *Maria will leave school next year. She's going to be a dental nurse.*

1 Dieter/leave school/next month/mechanic ....

2 Paolo/finish training/in 2 years/electrical engineer

3 Juliette/finish training/in 3 weeks/radio announcer

4 Oscar and Alfonso/stop working at the factory/next week/gardeners

4 Match Column **A** with Column **B**, then make questions and answers, like this:

How long does it take to boil an egg?
– It takes about four minutes.

A	B
boil an egg	four minutes
read a book	three and a half hours
remove a tooth	half an hour
fly to Paris from London	seven years
train to be a doctor	one hour

1 ....

2 ....

3 ....

4 ....

5 Complete this table and then fill in the gaps below.

verb	noun
choose	....
decide	....
discuss	....
....	marriage
....	training

1 I became a teacher because I enjoy teaching younger people. It was a good ....

2 In many countries women don't have a career. They get .... and work at home.

3 Some people are unable to .... anything. They are always right and never listen to anyone.

4 Look at this dress. Do you think I made the right .... ?

5 I haven't .... yet if I want to become a doctor or not. I don't know if I am the kind of person who can .... for so long.

42

Clamping down on tourists

1 Complete these words:

just____ wh__l c____p r__tric____

privi___g_ ru__ t__ris_ f_n_

tr____ic war____

2 Fill in the missing verbs in these sentences.

1 In Britain it is illegal to p............... your car on a double yellow line.

2 You can t............... somebody well, or badly.

3 Some people say the British b............... in fair play. Others disagree.

4 If you don't o............... the rules you might get a fine.

5 If you take something off, or take it away, you r............... it.

3 Complete these sentences, using *have to*, or *should* in the correct tense.

1 You shouldn't cross the road here, you .... cross at the lights.

2 If you are in the town you .... drive at under 60 kph.

3 When Roberto went to London he was clamped and .... pay a fine.

4 When you come to Britain you .... look to the right when you cross the road.

5 You .... park your car on a busy road.

6 When I was in Paris I .... drive very carefully.

4 Choose *ought to* or *have to*, and make sentences, like this:

clean your teeth every day
You ought to clean your teeth every day.

1 drive on the left in Britain

....

2 pay a fine when you get clamped

....

3 buy a ticket when you go by train

....

4 drive at or below the speed limit

....

5 check the oil in your car frequently

....

6 put out your cigarette at petrol stations

....

5 Choose *don't have to* or *mustn't*, and make sentences like this:

cross the road when you see a red man
You mustn't cross the road when you see a red man.

1 check your tyres every time you get in the car

....

2 clean the car every week

....

3 look in the mirror when you start your car

....

4 park on double yellow lines

....

5 drive on the right after landing in the UK

....

6 Think of driving rules and restrictions in your country, and make three sentences like this:

In .... you can ...., but you can't ....

1 ....

2 ....

3 ....

Social situations

1 Complete these words:

co__h   brain su____on   tha__

pref____nce   adv_c_   apolog____

ch___el   po__t_

2 Fill in the missing verbs in these sentences.

1   When you speak about something in passing, we can say that you m.................... it.

2   The verb *lend* is the opposite of b.................... .

3   When you put your foot down on something you s.................... on it.

4   When you want to say that you are sorry about something, you a.................... .

3 Rearrange these short dialogues, so that they make sense.

1   would/teacher/like/I/be/a/to. About/what/you?

....

– prefer/farmer/I'd/be/to/a

....

2   wonder/telephone/use/I/if/could/I/your?

....

– of/yes/course

....

3   mind/you/shut/if/I/door/the/would?

....

– at/not/all

....

4   much/thank/very/you

....

– mention/it/don't

....

4 Complete the following sentences. Use one of the verbs in the box in each sentence.

lend   borrow   open   close   go

1   Do you think I ....

2   Do you think we ....

3   I wonder if I ....

4   I wonder if you ....

5   Would you mind if I ....

5 Write answers for these questions.

1   Would you rather be a doctor or a dentist?

....

2   Would you mind if I arrived a little late?

....

3   Do you think I could borrow your newspaper?

....

4   Is this mine? Thank you very much.

....

6 What do you say in the following situations?

1   You push into someone on a bus, and apologise.

....

2   You want to borrow someone's pen.

....

3   Someone apologises to you for being late.

....

4   You are in waiting room at a railway station which is full of cigarette smoke.

....

Say it with movements

1 Complete these words:

di__g__e ext__me__ c__t__t_d

t_n_e amu____ ge__ur_ fr__n

pop_____ity

2 Fill in the verbs which are missing from the following sentences.

1 When you move something up and down, or from side to side you s.................... it.

2 When you transfer information successfully to another person, we say you c.................... .

3 The opposite of *like* is d.................... .

4 If you like something a lot then you e.................... it.

5 When you say hello to someone, you g.................... them.

3 Write sentences of your own to explain what makes you feel the following:

bored interested worried amused

I feel bored when I have to do something I dislike doing.

1 ....

2 ....

3 ....

4 ....

4 Rearrange the words to make sentences.

1 right/on/person/the/sitting/is/sister/the/my

....

2 woman/wearing/dress/blue/France/from/is/the/the

....

3 man/old/the/driving/the/is/father/my/car

....

5 Rewrite the sentences below, using *while* or *whereas*, like this:

In Argentina they speak Spanish, (Brazil/Portuguese)

In Argentina they speak Spanish whereas in Brazil they speak Portuguese.

1 Summer in Nepal is very wet. (winter/dry) ....

....

2 In Italy there are 50 million people. (Australia/8 million) ....

....

3 In Switzerland, the people speak 3 different languages. (Greece/only one) ....

....

4 If you shake your head in Britain, it means 'no'. (India/yes) ....

....

5 When you meet a friend in England you say 'hello'. (France/'bonjour') ....

....

6 Answer these questions:

1 What would you do if you found some money on the street?

I would ....

2 What would you do if a waiter spilt soup on your clothes?

....

3 What would you do if someone sat next to you on a train and turned his radio on very loudly?

....

4 What would you do if someone in a shop gave you the wrong change?

....

5

Cash in on our service

1 Complete these words:

acc___nt   bra__h   pers___l   con_____nt

cl_r_   fin___ci_l   ser____e   ins__anc_

2 Fill in the missing words in these sentences:

1 Instead of saying that we give a service we often say that we o............... it.

2 When you present an idea for the first time, we say that you i............... it.

3 Sometimes, when you give advice you s............... something to somebody.

4 When you give someone a cheque you have to s............... it in the right-hand corner.

5 If you want to get money, you c............... a cheque at a bank.

3 Match Columns A and B to write questions and answers, like this:

Who was the first person to reach the South Pole?
– It was Scott.

A	B
reach the South Pole	Neil Armstrong
run a mile in under four minutes	Scott
	Yuri Gagarin
climb Mount Everest	Sir Edmund Hillary
fly in space	Roger Bannister
walk on the moon	

1 ....

2 ....

3 ....

4 ....

4 Complete Column B by writing in a suitable verb, then make sentences by matching A and B, like this:

A bank is a place where you can cash money.

A	B
chemist's	*cash* ...... money
cash dispenser	.... stamps
restaurant	.... medicine
pub	.... money
bank	.... foreign currency
exchange bureau	.... a meal
post office	.... a drink

1 ....

2 ....

3 ....

4 ....

5 ....

6 ....

5 Complete the suggestions below.

1 I'm feeling really hungry.   L............ go to a ....

2 I think I've worked really hard this year.
   – W............ .... you take a .... ?

3 I'm quite thirsty but I'm not sure what to have.
   – W............ .... a cup of tea?

46

Becoming a woman in Japan

1 Complete these words:

su_na_e lib_____ted com__n pr___ab_y

ty_____l suc__s____l

adve_____ement eng_____ing

2 Fill in the missing verbs in these sentences.

1 Another word for *know* or *understand* is

r............... . You might say, 'I'm sorry I spoke

to you in French. I didn't r............... you were

English.'

2 If you l............... to something then you hear it.

3 If you get money for work you do, then you

e............... it.

4 Before you eat your meal, you p............... it.

5 In the past, women always used to stay at home to

l.......... a.......... the children.

3 Make sentences about your country, using the prompts below and *only*, *both . . . and* or *neither . . . nor*, like this:

vote *In my country both men and women are used to voting.*

1 go to college ....

....

2 study scientific subjects ....

....

3 look after children ....

....

4 wear trousers ....

....

5 go out in the evenings ....

....

4 Change these sentences, as in the example. Use *quite unusual* or *quite common* in your replies.

Not many people go windsurfing in Norway.

Windsurfing is quite unusual in Norway.

1 A lot of people drink coffee in the USA.

....

2 Very few people go skiing in Malaysia.

....

3 A lot of people go trekking in Nepal.

....

4 Most people in China eat rice.

....

5 Match Columns A, B and C to make sentences, like this:

Both Sabena and BA are airlines.

A	B	C
swimming	cycling	in South America
fruit	vegetables	*airlines*
Bob	Jack	contain vitamins
Sabena	*B A*	English names
Colombia	Peru	good exercise

1 ....

2 ....

3 ....

4 ....

7

47

Find a new you at the Slim Inn

1 Complete these words:

fr__nd_y   atm_____ere   cal_

cong___ial   di__   str___   del____ous

fi____ss   ov__w____ht

2 Fill in the missing verbs in these sentences.

1 If you decide what you are going to do in advance, you p.................... things carefully.

2 In the morning you get up, and then you g.................... d....................ed.

3 If you are made to leave your job – perhaps you've been a bad worker – we say you have been g....................en the s.................... .

4 If you want to know how heavy you are, then you w.................... yourself.

5 Another word for teach is i.................... .

3 Mary is a patient in hospital. Look at what happened to her yesterday, and make sentences, like this:

After Mary had been woken up, she was washed by the nurse.

6.30	wake up
7.00	wash by nurse
7.15	give injection
7.45	take to operating theatre
8.00	another injection
8.30	operate on
10.00	take back to hospital ward

....

....

....

....

....

....

....

4 Complete these sentences in your own words:

1 You might go to a pub because you feel like a ....

2 You might go to an Italian restaurant because you feel like a ....

3 .... because you feel like a holiday.

4 .... because you feel like a sleep.

5 What will you be doing tomorrow, next week, next month? Write sentences, describing what you will be doing, like this:

At five o'clock *I'll be going home.*

1 This evening ....

....

2 Tomorrow, at twelve o'clock, ...

....

3 Next Wednesday morning, ...

....

4 Next Sunday morning, ...

....

5 Next Christmas, ...

....

8

Eurochick

1 Complete these words:

jus___ce par_____me__t part____lar

mis____bl_ b_d___t inh___it___t

ba_____y ch____en

2 Fill in the verbs which are missing from these sentences.

1 A chicken l................ eggs. At least, some do.

2 Governments p................ laws.

3 A rise in food prices a................s us all, but especially the poor.

4 A mechanic in a garage may r................ your car if it has broken down.

5 If you take something away, then you r................ it.

3 Rewrite these sentences, using the passive infinitive.

The police need to investigate the report.

The report needs to be investigated.

1 They must build some more houses.

....

2 We have to employ more staff to deal with this.

....

3 We should discuss this problem.

....

4 They have to choose three students to appear on TV.

....

4 Make questions from the following, as in the example.

We've been watching a film.

What have you been watching?

1 They've been walking in the park.

....

2 They've been sailing in the Mediterranean.

....

3 We've been working at the library.

....

4 We've been jogging through the town.

....

5 They've been building another room for their house.

....

5 Make sentences, following the example.

watch TV   go for a walk   I

I don't know whether to watch TV or go for a walk.

1 have a cup of coffee   cup of tea   I

....

2 buy a paper   magazine   She

....

3 learn French   German   He

....

4 buy a Ford   BMW   They

....

5 go to a restaurant   eat at home   We

....

Newspapers: how objective are they?

1 Complete these words:

pol_____s   the a____   sour__

con____rence   dep_____en_

rep_____r   ob____tiv_   ed___or

2 Fill in the missing verbs in these sentences.

1 Another word for *make* or *manufacture*, is p............... .

2 If you have to decide whether something is good or bad, then you j............... it.

3 If you talk about a subject, and ask questions and give opinions about it, then you d............... it.

4 Another very common word for *journalist* is r............... .

5 When you get something ready, you p............... it.

3 Put the words below into the sentences.

by whom   for whom   about which (×2)   to whom
in which

1 That's a subject .... he knows nothing.

2 You have to think about the people .... the article is written.

3 He has no idea .... it was written.

4 These are the people .... it should go.

5 Do you think there are some subjects .... journalists shouldn't write?

6 That's the building .... the books are kept.

4 Change the following sentences, using *where* or *in which*.

For example: I park my car in that place.

That's the place where I park my car.

1 We stayed in that hotel. (in which)

....

2 They had the accident at that place. (where)

....

3 You can have really good food in this restaurant. (where)

....

4 They have very high unemployment in this town. (in which)

....

5 Change the sentences below into the passive, and complete the sentences which tell you where the action might happen.

For example: They open the mail at nine o'clock.

The mail is opened at nine o'clock.

I think this might happen in *an office.*

1 They check the tickets quite frequently.

....

I think this might happen on ....

2 They read through the articles very carefully.

....

I think this might happen in ....

3 They check the luggage extremely carefully.

....

I think this might happen in ....

10

50

Television

1 Complete these words:

pr_____bly   dra_a   com___y   new_

docum_____ar_   com_____cia_

info__at_____   cha__e_

2 Fill in the missing verbs in these sentences.

1 When you advertise on television you are trying to i..................... the way people think.

2 If you stop somebody from doing things, then we say that you r..................... that person.

3 Another verb which is similar in meaning to *happen* is o..................... .

4 If advertisements suddenly appear at an interesting part of a film, we can say that the advertisements i..................... the film.

3 The following words appear in Unit 20 in the Coursebook. Write another word in each case which has a similar meaning.

usually _____   rapidly _____

funny _____   tablets _____

dreadful _____   excellent _____

4 Add the word *that* to each of the following sentences:

1 The British public are used to programmes the government and advertisers cannot influence.

2 A recent survey shows that a famous soap opera is the programme people watched most.

3 Do television programmes really show things you want to see?

4 Thrillers are the films I enjoy most.

5 Which is the television channel you like best?

5 Match Columns A and B to produce sentences, using *in which*, *from which* and *on which*.

For example: *A sports review is a programme in which you expect to see some athletes.*

A	B
sports review	you expect to hear about world events
chat show	you expect to see some athletes
news broadcast	you expect to see adverts
documentary	you expect to see people talking
commercial channel	you expect to learn something

1 ....

2 ....

3 ....

4 ....

6 Write three sentences about things which you think *shouldn't be allowed* on television.

1 ....

2 ....

3 ....

7 Every country has certain restrictions. For example, in some countries alcohol *can't be advertised* on television. Write three sentences about things which *can't be done* in your country.

1 ....

2 ....

3 ....

Unlocking a legend

1 Complete these words:

h___o c_medi___ symb___ scre_n tra___

leg___d bio_____er favo____te

2 Fill in the missing verbs in these sentences:

1 When you feel pleasure or sadness, for example, we say that you are ex................ing these feelings.

2 If you lose hope about something, you are dis................ed.

3 Symbols are something which r................ something else.

4 A person may ask to borrow something from you. If you give it to this person, then you l................ it to them.

5 If you don't like something – for example, there may be a lot of noise in your hotel, or your meal in the restaurant may be bad – then you may c................ .

3 Complete these sentences in your own words:

1 I don't often go to ....

2 I hardly ever ....

3 In my family, we rarely ....

4 I frequently ....

5 .... quite often.

4 Change the following sentences, like this:

Could you lend me your pen? (He)

He asked me if I could lend him my pen.

1 Could I go outside? (She)

....

2 Could I have some more tea? (He)

....

3 Could I use your phone, please? (She)

....

4 Could I borrow your car for an hour? (He)

....

5 Could you tell me the time, please? (She)

....

5 Rewrite these questions with the correct word order:

1 close/ask/she/the window/didn't/you/to?

....

2 tell/you/do/to/what/he/did?

....

3 her/ask/what/they/did?

....

4 did/who/he/to/that/do/ask?

....

5 not/do/to/what/did/tell/her/they?

....

12

52

Seeing is believing

1 Complete these words:

im__e   po____r   bro__ure

mai_   ser___s   imp__tan__

vi____l   sy__ol   eff____ive

2 Fill in the missing verbs in these sentences.

1 When you see something and know it, then you r.............. it.

2 If you want people to know about a product you have to a................ it well.

3 If we look at something closely, we ex................ it.

4 If you say or write something in a much shorter way, you s................ise it.

5 Another word for influence is a................ .

3 One word in each list below does not belong to the list. The reason is that two words are negatives of adjectives but the third is not. Underline the word which does not belong to the list.

1 ineffective   interest   inexperienced

2 unsightly   unimportant   understand

3 improbable   impossible   impress

4 misunderstood   misused   mister

4 Write sentences of your own, using the prompts below:

For example: A fire *makes you warm.*

1 Medicine ....

2 Too much food ....

3 Too much to drink ....

4 Too little sleep ....

5 Too much sun ....

5 Make sentences from the prompts, like this:
The Eiffel Tower *makes me think of Paris.*

1 High mountains ....

2 People fishing ....

3 Men in leather trousers ....

4 Cloudy weather and rain ....

5 Men on camels ....

6 Make sentences from the prompts.

For example: very young/he/very good pianist

In spite of being very young he's a very good pianist.

1 rather old/she/can walk 20 km a day ....

2 very expensive/training course/not very effective ....

3 cheap/magazine/not very popular ....

4 very well advertised/car/not sell very well ....

5 carefully looked after/the video/not work very well ....

7 Complete the sentences below in your own words.

1 A computer is often used ....

2 A video is often used ....

3 Salt and pepper are often used ....

4 A diary is often used ....

5 Taxis are often used ....

13

53

A magnificent obsession with colour

1 Complete these words:

t__me   proc___s   meth__   tech___q_e

exh_b____on   t_ol   bas_c   mat____al

2 Fill in the missing verbs in these sentences.

1 When you show somebody how to do something you d.................. it.

2 If you want to change the colour of a piece of material, you can d.................. it.

3 If a town or organisation arranges an exhibition, or concert, or pop festival, we say that it p..................s o.................. an exhibition.

4 If you are very affected by something, we say that you are i.................. by it.

5 Writers of books write books, but writers of music c...................

3 Make sentences about the people in the chart.

Example: *Pedro was living in Madrid from January to December 1984. Before that, he had lived in Barcelona. Recently he has been working in the United States.*

	Before 1984	1984	Now
Pedro	live/Barcelona	live/ in Madrid	work/ United States
Ulla	work/ in Heidelberg	work/ in Bonn	be/ Düsseldorf
Ray	work/on a ship	work/ in an office	be/ unemployed
Jean	work/in a hotel	run/ a restaurant	work/ as a cook

1 Ulla ....

2 Ray ....

3 Jean ....

4 Rearrange the words to make good questions.

1 long/in/worked/have/Rome/you?

2 address/your/what's?

3 do/work/where/you?

4 influenced/he/by/teacher/his/was/very?

5 you/she/lived/can/remember/long/has/how/there?

6 living/she/been/there/has/she/was/since/born?

5 Look at the chart and write sentences, like this:

Martin likes modern art and James does too, but Mary has never really liked it.

	Martin	James	Mary
Likes modern art	√	√	x
Likes sculpture	√	x	√
Likes pop music	x	√	√
Likes batik	x	√	√

1 ....

2 ....

3 ....

14

54

Colour talks

1 Complete these words:

magn___   desig____   arch_____ct   dra___t_c

att___t___n   exp___t   fas_____able

c___plex__on

2 Fill in the missing verbs in these sentences.

1 Some people, or some events, may change your life enormously. We say that you are i................ed by them.

2 If someone keeps telling you how good you are, then we say that they f.................. you.

3 If you like a colour very much, or perhaps if you like a person because the colour of his or her clothes interests you, then we say that you are a...................ed.

4 Many things in life can change the way we feel or think. These things a.................. us.

3 Write sentences following the example:

    red car (like)   blue car

We don't like the red car but we do like the blue car.

1 large towns (like)   small towns ....
....

2 French cheese (like)   English cheese ....
....

3 the coast (go to)   mountains ....
....

4 classical music (enjoy)   pop music ....
....

4 Here are some sentences which can be written with the word *that*. Read them through and write them out including the word *that*.

1 That man I told you about is over there.
....

2 The village I lived in is now a large town.
....

3 We went into the church you visited.
....

5 These sentences are all incorrect. Rewrite them, including the word *who*, to make good sentences.

1 The man lives in that house is 84.
....

2 I saw the person runs the garage in the park.
....

3 Anybody writes on the walls should clean them.
....

15

55

Operation Raleigh

1 Complete these words:

adv_____e com_____ty cont_____t

des____ jun____ oc_a_ exp____men_

hu____d

2 Fill in the missing verbs in these sentences.

1 If something is very carefully chosen, then we say it is s..................ed.

2 When you arrange all the details, for a journey, for example, then you or.................... everything.

3 If you give money to something, then we say that you d.................... money.

4 Another word for *finished* is c..................ed.

5 Some ships use engines to help them cross the seas. Others don't. But we say that all ships s..................

3 Rewrite these questions with the correct word order.

1 it/has/ever/seen/been?

....

2 that/taught/you/ever/haven't/been/about?

....

3 explained/ever/hasn't/it/been?

....

4 been/adventurers/have/the/selected?

....

4 Complete these sentences in your own words.
For example: The Himalayas, *which are in Nepal and Tibet*, are the highest mountains in the world.

1 Greece, ... ,

is a good place for a holiday.

2 Paris, ... ,

has a population of several millions.

3 The River Amazon, ... ,

is thousands of kilometres long.

4 Madrid, ... ,

is the capital of Spain.

5 Make sentences from the chart.

	Athens	Corfu	Rome	Bologna
Bob and Andrew	✓	✓		
Gerhard			✓	✓
Delia	✓			✓
Rachel and Teresa		✓	✓	
Tom	✓		✓	

Bob and Andrew went not only to Athens, but also to Corfu.

1 ....

2 ....

3 ....

4 ....

6 Write three examples under each heading.

	deserts	oceans	mountain ranges
1	_____	_____	_____
2	_____	_____	_____
3	_____	_____	_____

16

Adopt an animal at London Zoo

1 Complete these words:

exc_____g wor___wh___e cha____

coll_____n wi___li___ rep_____

ad_____ion av___lable

2 Fill in the missing verbs in these sentences.

1 When you take care of a child who was not yours to begin with, we say that you a.................. that child.

2 If you look at something or someone and you know what it is, or who they are, then we use the verb r.................. .

3 Instead of using the verb *to telephone* someone, we sometimes use the verb to r.................. someone u.................. .

4 If you give somebody a ticket for a play or a film, and you don't ask them to pay, we say it is a c.................. ticket.

3 Make sentences about the following cities, like this:

Paris/biggest/Europe

Paris is one of the biggest cities in Europe.

1 Cairo/biggest/world

....

2 Florence/most beautiful/Europe

....

3 La Paz/highest/world

....

4 Stockholm/northernmost/world

....

5 Montevideo/southernmost/world

....

4 Look at the chart and make sentences about the likes and dislikes of the people on the left.

Example: *James dislikes sailing, and so does Eric.*

	sailing	fishing	swimming	walking	climbing	windsurfing
James	x	✓	x	✓	x	
Amanda	✓	x			✓	✓
Tom	✓	x	x	x	x	
Eric	x		✓		x	✓

1 ....

2 ....

3 ....

4 ....

5 ....

5 Listen to the tape, and answer the questions.

6 Reply to these questions giving a description of the animal.

What's a badger? *It's a black and white animal that comes out at night.*

1 What's a reptile? ....

2 What's a camel? ....

3 What's a cockatoo? ....

4 What's a koala bear? ....

5 What's a kangaroo? ....

A kind of medicine

1 Complete these words:

conv__t__nal   alt__nat__e

nutr_____nal   med__a__   orth__ox

pat__nt   surv__   dep__ssion   anx__ty

2 Fill in the verbs which are missing from the following sentences.

1 These days doctors have to t............... many patients who are suffering from stress.

2 Since 1969, many doctors have c............... their minds about alternative medicine.

3 If you are very depressed, we say that you s............... from depression.

4 When you visit the doctor, he will probably p............... some medicine for you.

5 When you want to get the juice from a lemon you s............... it.

3 Complete these columns.

noun	verb	adjective
	believe	—
nutrition	—	
medicine	—	
	meditate	—
healing		
tension	—	
	—	anxious
	treat	—

4 Make statements as in the example.

suffer/from depression/she – insomnia

She didn't suffer from depression but she did suffer from insomnia.

1 suffer/from headaches/he – backaches

....

2 know/about the new treatment/she – acupuncture

....

3 learn/about the new methods/they – hypnotherapy

....

4 feel/very worried/he – angry

....

5 smoke/cigarettes/he – cigars

....

5 Complete these sentences in your own words, as in the example.

He eats six times a day, which *is far too much.*

1 She smokes forty cigarettes a day, which ....

2 I only sleep four hours a night, which ....

3 He drives nearly two thousand km a week, which ....

4 He was given £100 but I was only given £10, which ....

5 He earns £100,000 a year, which ....

6 Some people can't find work, which ....

7 Some people behave very badly at football matches, which ....

8 He speaks very slowly, which ....

9 Her English is extremely good, which ....

58

Movers   How mobile are you?

1 Complete these words:

mo__le   esp_____ll_   sic_____ss

adver___s__g   sci_____is_   inc___di_g

jet l__   tho____nds

2 Fill in the missing verbs in these sentences.

1 If you have a sickness or an illness very often, then we say that you s............... from it.

2 If you are the head of a company or business then we say that you r............... it.

3 When you go from one town to another and have to change homes, then we say that you m............... house.

4 If you go to a school, then we can say that you a...............d it. The same word is also used when you go to a meeting.

3 Make four sentences from the chart.

	occupation	parents	interests	home town
Megan	nurse	Cardiff	reading mountaineering	Swansea
Liana	teacher	Florence	travel foreign languages	Milan
Peter	unemployed	Liverpool	training dogs sailing	Manchester

Megan, who lives in Swansea, likes reading and mountaineering.
Megan, whose parents live in Cardiff, lives in Swansea.

1 ....

2 ....

3 ....

4 ....

4 Follow these instructions to answer the questions.

1 Add the following numbers, except for the second and the last. 6, 19, 45, 37, 2, 6 = _____

2 Add the following numbers, except for the first and the fifth. 19, 22, 2, 4, 6, 98, 5 = _____

3 If you add the number of days in each month together, not including February, what is the answer? _____

5 Rewrite these questions with the correct word order.

1 planes/on/how/have/many/been/you?

....

2 anyone/know/does/she/who/from/suffers/sea/sickness?

....

3 been/to/you/have/countries/Asia/in/any?

....

4 often/house/how/you/do/move?

....

19

59

Missing

1 Complete these words:

orga_____t_o_   ident_____ti_n

cer_____cat_   li_____ce   dis__p___

pas_p____

2 Fill in the missing verbs in these sentences.

1 When you make a book and sell it to the public, you p............ the book.

2 Imagine you see a robbery, and you see the robber, but he runs away. Later, the police ask you to look through a group of photographs. If you see the robber, and you can say to the police, 'yes, that's the man', then you have i..............ied the person.

3 Another word for *permit* or *allow* is l............ .

4 If you have no money, and have a lot of bills to pay, you are very unhappy, and you probably w............ a lot about how to pay the bills.

5 The opposite of *dead* is a............ .

3 Read the following passage and put in the word *who*, *which* or *whose*.

The parents .... child went missing live near Drayton, ... is a small village near the coast. Very few people live in the area, ... is well known for its thick woods and sudden mists from the sea. The young boy, ... is a quiet child, likes playing by himself, and only rarely goes very far from his parents' farm, ... is about 200 metres off the main road. Police have asked neighbours to help in the search.

4 One of the words in each list below does not belong in the list. Underline the word which does not belong, and explain why, like this:

passport   <u>milk carton</u>   driving licence   ID card
They can all identify you, except for milk carton.

1 cheque   credit card   address book   money

They can all buy things, ...

2 handbag   briefcase   paper bag   poster

They are all used for carrying things, ...

....

3 driving licence   passport   photograph   visa

They all allow you to do things, ...

5 Rearrange these sentences, and then decide to whom you might say each one.

1 hope/tomorrow/let/he'll/me/leave/early/I

....

2 won't/let/go/why/me/you?

....

3 drive/me/let/please

....

4 could/you/know/let/them/that/late/we/be/will

....

5 let/don't/cook/it/long/too

....

20

TAPESCRIPT

1

7 A reporter is interviewing some people about unusual sports.

Interviewer Hello, Andrea. I've just been watching you skiing. You're really very good, aren't you? Very fast indeed.
Andrea Thank you. I <u>do</u> teach skiing, you know, so I have to be good. But now I also have to be very fast, because I've been selected for the Olympic team and I'm training for the Olympic Games next year.
Interviewer Photos, water sports are your work – waterskiing, parasailing . . . Do you still enjoy them?
Photos Oh yes, I love waterskiing particularly, but some days, when it's raining, there's nothing to do. So I'm learning to play chess in my spare time. It's a nice game, you know . . .
Interviewer And Yannis, how old are you?
Yannis I'm fifteen. I'm on holiday at the moment and I'm helping my brother. I'm learning to drive the boat. But I live in Athens with my family. I'm a student there.
Interviewer Claude, you look very fit. How old are you?
Claude I'm fifty now. I own this windsurfing club, but I'm also the club manager. I windsurf a lot and I meet a lot of British and Canadians, so I'm studying English twice a week – in the evenings.
Interviewer Stewart – you're from Scotland, aren't you?
Stewart Yes, I'm a bank manager in Aberdeen. But as you know, I go underwater caving. I want to go to Borneo next summer. But it's a very dangerous sport so I'm practising diving every weekend, at the moment.

2

1

Markham When is your birthday, Jennifer?
Jennifer In April. I'm seven and a half.
Markham You live with your mother and father, do you?
Jennifer Only Mummy. Mummy and Daddy are divorced. But I see Daddy at weekends.
Markham What do you like to do?
Jennifer Oh, I like everything.
Markham I mean specially. What do you like to do at weekends?
Jennifer I like the seaside, I like going to the farm. And the shops . . .
Markham What are you going to do when you grow up?
Jennifer Oh, I'm going to be a dancer. A ballerina. And a wife. I'm going to have a husband, and lots of children, and a horse, and lots of dogs and cats.

3

Jennifer A dancer? Did I say that? Yes, of course. Now I remember.
Markham And what <u>do</u> you do?
Jennifer Well, my father wanted me to be a doctor, like he was. And I wanted . . . well, I guess I wanted to please him. And so here I am – a doctor, almost.
Markham How long does it take then . . . to become a doctor?
Jennifer It takes seven or eight years.
Markham That's a long time. And it's difficult, isn't it?
Jennifer Yes, it's difficult. In fact, the last seven years haven't been easy at all. I'm divorced, you see. I've got a little boy, but he lives with his father and I hardly see him. He's in France. I married over there before I started studying, and it didn't work. But I've remarried since.
Markham What about your father?
Jennifer My father? He died, oh, about four years ago.

3

1

Reporter Excuse me, Madam. Is that your car?
Gina Yes, I'm afraid it is.
Reporter It's been clamped, hasn't it?
Gina Yes. I've just been to Harrods to collect a dress, and I was only gone for about ten minutes.
Reporter Are you angry?
Gina Of course I'm angry. Well, I suppose I shouldn't park in a no parking zone. I took a chance, but I was away for such a short time.
Reporter But why did you park there?
Gina Well, you know . . . you can't find a parking place in London. I drove around for twenty minutes and then I parked here. I had to collect my dress and meet a friend. Now I'm late, of course.
Reporter What happens next?
Gina I don't know. I'll have to phone the police, I suppose.

6

Have you seen this letter from the Italian tourist, Mrs Coppola?
– Yes, I have. She seemed very angry.
Yes, I think she was. Well, I've written a reply. Listen. Do you think it's all right?
Dear Mrs Coppola
Thank you for your letter of 26th April. I am sorry that you had a bad time in London. I imagine that you parked on a double yellow line. I'm afraid in London you mustn't do that. We have to use clamps because there are too many cars in London and so little room for parking. Sometimes we give tickets but people just don't pay their fines. I hope you . . .

4

5

1	Do you think I could borrow five pounds?	– Don't mention it.
2	You'd better stop taking sleeping pills.	– Not at all.
3	Would it be possible to pay by cheque?	– Of course, Sir.
4	Would you mind if my friend stayed the night?	– Certainly.
5	May I borrow your radio?	– Yes, of course.
6	I'm really terribly sorry.	– Don't mention it.
7	Thanks.	– I don't mind.

8

1 Oh, gosh I <u>am</u> sorry.
2 Would it be possible to turn your radio down a bit?
3 Not at all.
4 What about you?
5 Don't mention it.
6 I wonder if you could close the door.

5

6

I had this experience only a few days ago. I was at a party at a friend's house and I was introduced to a man I had never met before. His name was James, or maybe John. James – that's right. James Bacon. Now most people stand a metre or so away from each other when they are talking, but he didn't. He came right up to me. We were almost touching. The room was nearly empty and I moved back, but he followed. I moved again, and again he followed. But I don't think he knew he was doing it. I don't think he knew at all. Perhaps other people wouldn't feel anything in that situation, but for me it was terrible.

6

3

If you ask someone, they'll say that the bank is where you can cash a cheque. But it's more than that and we have to tell people that in our advertisements. There are several things to think about. When do you start? I mean at what age. That is the first problem. I think you must start very young. So <u>we</u> said: 'Let's introduce the name of the bank to children and they will never forget it.' The next question is this: How do you attract the different age groups? My partner said 'Why don't we use a gimmick for each age group? Give them something for nothing – money boxes for young children, T-shirts for teenagers, gold pens for young executives.' That always works. But what

62

do you give to your best customer? That's another question. What about leather diaries, for example?

Banks are very competitive. How do you think of something new? That's always a problem. We were one of the first banks to have drive-in banks and to open on Saturdays, but now many banks do. Of course, most banks now offer insurance and travel services, and all the usual standing order and direct debit services. The other thing about advertising is where. Where do you put the ads – on television, of course, but which journals and newspapers? And when and how often? These are questions you have to ask yourself.

7

Clerk	Yes sir, can I help you?
Mario	Yes, can you cash a cheque for me, please?
Clerk	For how much?
Mario	For £150.
Clerk	I'm afraid we can't cash more than £75. Unless we call your bank, that is. And have you got a Eurocheque card?
Mario	Yes, here it is.
Clerk	That's fine. Could you sign the cheque on the back, please?
Mario	Yes. Today is the eleventh, isn't it?
Clerk	Yes, it is. How would you like it?
Mario	Sorry? Could you repeat that please?
Clerk	How would you like the money? Fives, tens, twenties?
Mario	Oh, tens please, and could you also tell me . . .

10

First write the date in the top right-hand corner. Today it's 17th March. You know the year, don't you? Make the cheque payable to J Smith & Sons, plc. The amount is nineteen pounds and fourteen pence. Write the amount in words on the lines below J Smith & Sons. Write the amount in figures in the box. Don't forget to sign your name in the bottom right-hand corner.

7

2

I had a working mother when I was a young girl. She went back to work when I was ten and my brother was fourteen. She taught at a school of dress design. I studied English at university. Then I got a job with an advertising agency as an assistant. I studied English so I could get a good job with a good company. In 1980 I went abroad with a friend. We spent a month in California. Then I worked for a company which sold cassette tapes and books for English conversation. I was still single at twenty-five, then my parents started to worry because their daughter wasn't married. Our neighbours and relations were asking when I would marry and they began to talk about an arranged marriage. In Japan they don't force you to marry someone, but they may give you a chance to meet someone. I am very interested in jazz and I met my husband in a jazz club. My parents didn't want their daughter to marry a foreigner. They didn't want me to come to England, but now I work in London for a Japanese newspaper.

4

Interviewer	Was having a working mother typical?
Momoko	No, it was rare, but she had a skill. She went to work when I was ten and my brother was fourteen.
Interviewer	And you went to university?
Momoko	Yes, I studied English at university.
Interviewer	Is that unusual?
Momoko	No, it's quite common. Japanese girls study English to get a good job with a good company.
Interviewer	Then you worked for a while?
Momoko	Yes, in an advertising agency. Most Japanese girls work before they get married.
Interviewer	And you travelled?
Momoko	Yes. In 1980 I went abroad with a friend. We spent a month in California.
Interviewer	Do many young Japanese women travel abroad?
Momoko	Yes, a lot do. They work and save money for marriage and for travel. They want to travel before they marry, because after that they won't have the chance.

Interviewer What happened then?
Momoko I worked for a company which sold cassette tapes and books for English conversation.
Interviewer Then you met your husband?
Momoko Yes. I am very interested in jazz and I met my husband at a jazz club.
Interviewer Were your parents glad that you were getting married?
Momoko Well, most Japanese women marry earlier than I did, but my parents didn't want their daughter to marry a foreigner. They didn't want me to come to England. Now I work in London for a Japanese newspaper.
Interviewer So you are a career woman, not a housewife. Are there other Japanese women in London like you?
Momoko There are a few, but not many.

8

1

Are you counting calories because you want to be slimmer? Do you feel like a change? Then get with it. Take off those extra pounds, tone up your muscles and find a new you in the friendly atmosphere and fresh mountain air at our Slim Inn. It's the only fun and fitness resort in the Rocky Mountains. It's a complete health programme of fun, fitness and personal development with six nights' accommodation and three daily meals plus lots of activities and sports. To find out more ring Freefone 403 225 9731 or write to Slim Inn, PO Box 888, Lake Louise, Alberta, Canada.

7

Pat is talking to one of the doctors at the Slim Inn.

Doctor Now then, Pat, you agree that you're overweight. Why do you think that you are?
Pat Well. I suppose I eat too much. Um, well, seriously, I . . . I don't eat regular meals and I eat a lot of chocolate, yes when I'm upset I eat chocolate. And if I feel tense I drink quite a lot – to relax.
Doctor So you have bad eating habits, which lead to gaining weight?
Pat That's right.
Doctor Why don't you eat regular meals?
Pat I never eat breakfast. And if I'm busy I don't eat lunch. Sometimes I don't even eat supper until nine or ten at night.
Doctor Why don't you make time to eat?
Pat There's a lot of pressure at work. I always feel under stress.
Doctor And why is that?
Pat It's a symptom of too much work, I suppose. I have to work very long hours, and when I feel that I've got too much to do I start to panic.
Doctor So overwork leads to stress.
Pat Yes, for everyone. And because I'm under stress, I never have enough time and my eating habits are bad. I guess it's all part of big city life.
Doctor You mean you are overweight because of urban living?
Pat Yes, yes, I think so. That and my job. I think if I lived in the country or had an easier job I would relax more easily and then I'd eat properly. Nobody who works like me can really relax.

9

5

Firstly, there is the Commission. This is responsible for general policies. There are 17 Commissioners, one from each of the member countries and two from the larger ones. These Commissioners decide whether to put forward a policy or not. They are based in Brussels.
Then there is the European Parliament, which is based in Strasbourg, and which has nearly 600 members. The Parliament decides whether it will accept the Community budget or not. The Council of Ministers takes the final decision on whether to accept proposals or not. Each country has one seat on the Council. For important policies, all twelve member countries must agree. The Court of Justice has judges from all countries, and they make decisions about the laws of the Community.

10

1 Each of the countries used to charge taxes on any goods moving between the countries. These taxes have now been removed, in order to allow more goods and cheaper goods in each country, and a better standard of living for the Community population.
2 All citizens of the Community are or will be free to look for work in any Community country. Work permits are not necessary.

3 There are common prices for food, to create equality in each country, and to make sure that the farmers earn enough money.
4 The Common Market gives money to regions with economic difficulties. Special help is given to the coal and steel industries, and to help in developing industry in the poorer areas.

10

2

A newspaper has a complex hierarchy. The easiest way to show this is in the form of a chart:
At the top of the chart there are four major positions. These are the Executive Editor, who talks to the unions and deals with legal and financial questions. Then there is the actual Editor of the paper and his deputy. The Editor makes decisions about what goes into the paper. The deputy has close contact with the House of Commons and the political content. Finally there is the Managing Editor, who sees that everything runs smoothly. Below this there are three Assistant Editors and the heads of the five departments. Each of the three Assistant Editors has a different responsibility. For example, one is responsible for design. The five departments are City News, which deals with financial matters, then Home, Foreign, Sports and Features. Features are the special sections including films, books and the Woman's page. So on the second level there are three Assistant Editors and the five Department Heads. Also on this level is the Night Editor. He looks after the paper, especially the front page, in the afternoon and evening, preparing material for publication the next morning. Below the second level there are the reporters and specialists, who write the reports and articles, and the sub-editors, who check and prepare the copy for the printer. There is also full secretarial back-up.

11

1

If someone tells you you have to watch the news on Channel Four and the play on Channel Two this evening, will you do it? You probably think you have the right to choose the programmes you like. But how much choice do we really have? Do television channels really show the things you want to see? Or do you sometimes watch things on TV you would never watch in the cinema or in the theatre?

7

Two people are talking about TV in Europe.

Woman ... but I thought that most European countries had both commercial and non-commercial channels?
Man No, not at all. Nine countries have commercial channels only.
Woman And how many channels do these have?
Man Well, nearly all of these nine have a choice of two channels, except France, which has three, and Luxembourg, which has only one.
Woman What about countries with non-commercial channels only?
Man There are only four of these. Two have only one channel, Sweden has two channels and Belgium has four.
Woman Oh, and what about countries which have...

12

6

An actress is talking about her director.
If you think I'm working for him again then you're wrong. First he told me to be in London on Monday, then five minutes later he told me <u>not</u> to go to London. Instead, he asked me to go to Paris. I said, 'What about London?' Then he said to me that I shouldn't question him. No, not shouldn't – couldn't. He actually said that I couldn't question him. He said he was the director – not me. I'll never work for him again. I promise you. In fact tomorrow I'm packing my bags and I'm catching the first train home. I'm walking off this set and out of his life.

8

Arthur, don't put the lamp there. No one will see it. You should read the plan first and then I would not have to tell you. Arthur? Are you deaf? Will you put the lamp on the table, where it's meant to be... Anne, you're excited. Could you speak more quickly? Yes, quickly. You're excited and I want people to know you're excited. And don't look at the floor. You're talking to your mother. Your mother's not lying on the floor, is she? Right, let's try it again.

13

4

Manager: Well, we had three products, all for women. The first was a range of lipstick with fifteen different colours. The second was a hair shampoo. The third was a very high quality face cream. In spite of the cost we chose to advertise on TV for the shampoo.

Interviewer: That's very expensive, I suppose?

Manager: Yes, the cost was very high and I'm not going to tell you how much. But we wanted to reach a wide group of people, and we needed movement, action, colour. Television had to be the medium.

Interviewer: Did you advertise the lipstick on TV, too?

Manager: No. Well, the lipstick was for the younger market, where we felt we could sell a lot. But the product was not expensive and we didn't want to spend too much money. So we chose poster advertising, and some advertising in magazines for younger women. And for the face cream we chose high quality magazines, in spite of the fact that not so many people read them. We didn't use TV, or posters, just this one medium. You see it's an expensive cream and we had to attract the right kind of woman. In spite of this, the campaign was really successful. Well, you know it was don't you?

7

Ours is a very expensive perfume. When people see it or hear the name we want them to think of luxury. There are many ways to do this. You show a woman in a fur coat, in a silk evening dress, maybe covered in diamonds. You can show an expensive car, an expensive restaurant, or a man in a tuxedo. We decided to do something different. We show a beautiful woman, simply but elegantly dressed, beside a series of paintings by Leonardo da Vinci, and it works. Because she is wearing the perfume, and because she is next to expensive and beautiful paintings, our perfume must be beautiful and expensive too. It does work.

14

3

Batik has been used for centuries in Asia and parts of Africa to create designs on cloth. Painters use wax and dye to make beautiful paintings and wall hangings. The basic method is this: first, parts of the cloth are covered in hot wax. The most common tools for this are brushes and copper spouts. After this the cloth is dyed. Then the wax is removed, and in those places where the wax was, the cloth remains unmarked. This is the basic method, but it can be changed in a number of ways.

8

That one is batik. A friend of mine invited me to make some pots on a wheel with clay. I worked all morning but I couldn't do it so I made this piece instead.
This is a piece about some people in the United States. Short legs and a hole in the head. Suffering fools.
This is the most recent painting. I tried to see what strange creatures I could paint. They all have fangs, claws or something to hunt each other. I think this says something about the times we live in.
This is another batik. It is one of my first successful batiks. Half of it was a bit of an accident, but I slowly added to it. It's a garden people plant in order to prevent rabbits from finding the real garden.
This batik was inspired by a postage stamp that I got on a letter from Switzerland after I had been in the United States for three years and away from Switzerland for more than six years.
This is watercolour and pen on cotton. They were, and still are, building a subway near our house. I thought about how this period will not last, so I drew a bulldozer as a separate piece on top of a landscape. The eye can easily take the bulldozer off the painting and imagine the scene without it.

15

1

Samantha Peters, a dress designer, talks about the effect you create by wearing different colours.

Interviewer: Let's start with black, for example. If black is the colour you choose to wear, what are you saying?

Samantha: Black is very grown up, it's very sophisticated. Black is the colour people choose in order to look older. Everyone can wear black. But you should wear more make-up and add colour in other ways, if you wear black.

Interviewer: And at the opposite end of the spectrum – white, that is.

Samantha	White stands for purity, fragility. It looks warm and wonderful in winter, cool and comfortable in summer. Everyone can wear it – it's very flattering.
Interviewer	And, halfway between – grey.
Samantha	Grey is, above all, business-like. You know the expression, 'the man in the grey flannel suit'. But, like black, if grey is the colour you choose, you should wear other colours with it.
Interviewer	What else is there, between the two extremes?
Samantha	Well, there's midnight blue, another name for navy, which is popular for sailors and school uniforms, but it is also very fashionable and it looks very smart with white and red. If this is a combination you like, don't put them together in equal amounts or you'll look like the French flag.
Interviewer	What about some brighter colours? What is the colour you should choose when you want attention?
Samantha	If you *don't* want attention wear brown. If you do want to be noticed, wear red.
Interviewer	And what about pink?
Samantha	It's the same really. Pink is a magnet. It's the colour you should wear if you want attention and admiration. Experts who study the psychology of colours say that pale pink is romantic and soft.
Interviewer	Another dramatic colour is gold, of course. Isn't it a colour you should only wear at night?
Samantha	Not any more. Gold is gorgeous and precious. It can be worn by blondes, redheads or brunettes and it can go anywhere, anytime.
Interviewer	Another warm colour is wine, I believe?
Samantha	Yes. It used to be called wine or maroon, but now it's called burgundy, named after Burgundian wine, of course. It's a colour you associate with royalty and it looks lovely against both light and dark skins, and with every colour of hair.

4

Every colour has a meaning. And as you choose a colour, you might like to remember that it's saying something. We've said that red is lovable. Green, on the other hand, stands for hope; it is tranquil. Pink is romantic, while brown is serious. White is an easy one – white is pure. Orange is generous. Violet is mysterious, turquoise is strong and blue is definitely feminine.

6

seagrass	Grand Turk
Middle Caicos	North Caicos
Grand Bahama	Lucayan National Park
fish breeding	Turks and Caicos Islands

Now listen to the news update.
In both Grand Bahama and the Turks and Caicos Islands the main objective is marine biology. The experiments in fish breeding have been successful, and so has the survey on seagrass. Seagrass is very important for the survival of many marine animals. In the Lucayan National Park there have been some delays, but the paths have been completed. In the Turks and Caicos Islands, the basketball court on North Caicos has not yet been finished, but the main work on a youth centre on Grand Turk has been done. On Middle Caicos sea divers are working on aircraft and ships which have been sunk. Divers have already found fourteen wrecks of old ships, and a much more modern aircraft belonging to the United States navy.

8

Operation Raleigh is funded by voluntary donations, and the adventurers are asked to find sponsors in the areas where they live. In fact many branches of commerce and industry have sent their young employees on Operation Raleigh – and they have paid for them completely. Included in this group are banks, electronic companies, engineering and building companies. Often equipment and food is received as a donation, and of course, the Operation also receives donations from individuals throughout the world.

17

3

London Zoo is one of the most famous zoos in the world. Together with Whipsnade Zoo it forms Britain's National Zoological Collection. It has no money of its own and relies on you for its support. Many of its animals are now in danger or are difficult to keep and breed in captivity. And most of them are very expensive to feed. So if you adopt an animal it'll not only help us, but it'll also make your own visits more enjoyable. And here's another thought: if you adopt an animal it may make a very special present for someone, whether for birthday, anniversary or Christmas.

8

Office	I'll just complete the form for you, if I may. Let's see. May I have your name and address, please?
Mrs Harrison	Yes, Harrison. With two r's. Mrs Anita Harrison.
Office	And your address?
Mrs Harrison	29 Emmerdale Road, London, SW12.
Office	And what is your telephone number, please?
Mrs Harrison	01 033 7293
Office	And is this a gift?
Mrs Harrison	Yes. Yes it is. It's for my granddaughter.
Office	What is her name?
Mrs Harrison	It's Alison . . . Alison Harrison.
Office	Do you want a special date on the certificate?
Mrs Harrison	Yes, I do. It's for her birthday, 6th January.
Office	Which animal or animals would you like to adopt?
Mrs Harrison	I want three animals. I'd like one duck. That's £10 isn't it? And one wallaby.
Office	Yes that's £30 for one unit.
Mrs Harrison	And a giraffe. That's £30 for one unit as well, isn't it?
Office	Yes, that's right. And would you like to pay by cheque, or cash?
Mrs Harrison	Oh, I'll pay cash, right now.
Office	Fine. That's £70. And would you like a complimentary entrance ticket or a season ticket reduction?
Mrs Harrison	Oh, a complimentary ticket please, so I can bring my granddaughter to see her adopted animals.

18

3

A doctor analyses the results of a survey on the changing patterns of belief in alternative medicine among members of his profession.

This survey definitely showed that doctors have changed their minds about alternative medicine. We split the group into older doctors – those who qualified before 1969, and rather younger doctors, those who qualified in 1970 or after. In the first group 17% disbelieved, 11% had a strong disbelief and the rest a slight disbelief. A large percentage didn't believe but they didn't disbelieve either – 24%. More than half of the doctors believed, but the majority of these had only a slight belief. In the younger group just over half the doctors had a slight belief. The number of those who had a strong belief, or those who didn't believe or disbelieve was almost the same; those with a strong belief were slightly higher. There were twice as many doctors with a slight disbelief as those with a strong disbelief. And the smallest percentage didn't know.

8

There are many remedies for bad breath. You can make a cup of peppermint tea – just put a teaspoon of fresh or dried mint in a cup and cover it with water. Then add a drop of lemon juice and drink it. Or, if you're in a hurry, you can chew parsley.
For colds it always does you good to drink hot honey and lemon juice before you go to bed.
You can use garlic cream for cuts. They used garlic on wounds in the First World War.
For nausea, when you feel sick, hot milk and honey with a bit of cinnamon can help a lot.
If you have very bad depression you should go to the doctor, but if you are depressed after an illness, eating oats will do you good.
If you have earache you can squeeze a few drops of lemon juice on a piece of cotton and plug your ear with it.
The juice of half an orange or onion juice is good for hiccoughs, and lime tea is beneficial when you can't sleep.
Sage tea with vinegar doesn't taste very nice, but it's good for a sore throat.
And if you feel sick in a car or plane, try powdered ginger.

19

2

Mary When we were first married I used to count the number of days. You know, 140 days one year, 160 another year. He travelled 140,000 miles one year, 180,000 another. But I don't count any longer.
Interviewer Does your husband not suffer from jet lag at all?
Mary Jet lag? He used to suffer a bit but now he says that he doesn't believe it really exists.
Interviewer Does all of his travelling worry you?
Mary I used to worry all the time. I always used to imagine he'd had an accident if he was late. I used to think he was married to the company – not me. Quite often when he comes home now somebody from the office is waiting for him at the airport with another ticket. So he doesn't even come home then. He just gets on the next plane out.

8

Interviewer Chris, you are an engineer and you travel a lot don't you?
Chris Yes, that's right. We seem to move every four or five years.
Interviewer How many States have you lived in so far?
Chris Well, let's see. First we lived in California, in San Diego, then it was Maryland. After that we went to Atlanta, Georgia – that's a lovely place. We didn't want to leave but my husband lost his job and we returned to California, I think. Yes, that's right. And then here to Colorado. Last year we went to New York, but that was only for three months. So we've lived in five States including New York.
Interviewer What does your husband do?
Chris He's a teacher, so he can get work quite easily.
Interviewer Have you ever travelled abroad?
Chris No, we've never been out of the States.

20

3

Mrs X I woke up in a strange bed. The light was very bright and it hurt my eyes. There was a woman, who was wearing a white cap, near the bed and a man who had a white coat and something round his neck.
Interviewer Do you have any problems when you talk?
Mrs X Oh . . . yes. At first I could hardly speak. I couldn't remember the words for 'knife' and 'fork', for instance, . . . or 'toothbrush'. It was very, very strange.
Interviewer What are you going to do now?
Mrs X I really don't know. I can't remember my name or anything about my job or family, if I had one. When the police found me, I was wandering about – in the middle of a main road. I didn't know where I was.
Interviewer Didn't you have a driving licence with you?
Mrs X No, I didn't have a driving licence.
Interviewer Didn't you have any identification? A cheque book, credit cards, photographs, keys – anything?
Mrs X There was nothing. Nothing at all, except for this.
Interviewer What's that?
Mrs X It's a silver necklace, which says 'Ron 1982'. It comes from Mexico.

6

1 We put photographs in papers they might read.
2 Next, we might try friends or relatives they might be with.
3 Often the person we are looking for has been in an accident.
4 We can put posters in places they might be.
5 We try to find the last person they saw or were with.

7

The first thing they do is to put out an APB and this goes to all the police stations in the country. Next we contact the hospitals. Often the person we are looking for has been in an accident. Then we might try parents, friends or relatives they might be with. We try to follow their movements and to find the last person they saw or were with. Then we try the media. We put photographs in local or national papers – especially papers they might read. There are other things we can do: put posters in places they might be, go on television. Here in America there is a magazine in which there are photographs of missing children. This is often the last hope. Of course, with nearly two million missing children every year, we can't do all these things for everyone. We haven't got the time, the money or the staff.